# Ed Parker's

# INFINITE INSIGHTS *INTO* KENPO

# INSIGHTS

## *VOLUME 5*

# MENTAL & PHYSICAL APPLICATIONS

*by*

# ED PARKER

Printed in the United States of America
Library of Congress Catalog Number 82-72784
First Printing June, 1987


ISBN 0-910293-10-4 (5 Volume Set)
ISBN 0-910293-09-0 (Volume 5 - cloth)
ISBN 0-910293-08-2 (Volume 5 - paper)


DELSBY PUBLICATIONS
Los Angeles, California

# TABLE OF CONTENTS

ACKNOWLEDGEMENTS. . . . . . . . . . . . . . . . . . . . . . . . . . . . . . . . . . . . . . . . . . . . iii
DEDICATION . . . . . . . . . . . . . . . . . . . . . . . . . . . . . . . . . . . . . . . . . . . . . . . . . iv
BLACK BELTPLEDGE . . . . . . . . . . . . . . . . . . . . . . . . . . . . . . . . . . . . . . . . v
ABOUT THE PLEDGE. . . . . . . . . . . . . . . . . . . . . . . . . . . . . . . . . . . . . . . . .vi
PREFACE . . . . . . . . . . . . . . . . . . . . . . . . . . . . . . . . . . . . . . . . . . . . . . . . . . .vii
CHAPTER 1 -- INTRODUCTION . . . . . . . . . . . . . . . . . . . . . . . . . . . . . . 1
CHAPTER 2 -- IMPORTANCE OF BASICS . . . . . . . . . . . . . . . . . . . . . . 7
CHAPTER 3 -- BASICS IN MOTION. . . . . . . . . . . . . . . . . . . . . . . . . . . . 11
                1. Short Form 1 . . . . . . . . . . . . . . . . . . . . . . . . . . . . . . . . . 13
                   a. What it Contains and Teaches. . . . . . . . . . . . . . . . 13
                2. Long Form 1 . . . . . . . . . . . . . . . . . . . . . . . . . . . . . . . . 22
                   a. What it contains and teaches. . . . . . . . . . . . . . . . . . 22
                3. Short Form 2 . . . . . . . . . . . . . . . . . . . . . . . . . . . . . . . . 40
                   a. What it contains and teaches. . . . . . . . . . . . . . . . . . 40
CHAPTER 4 -- PRIORITIES OF SELF-DEFENSE . . . . . . . . . . . . . . . . . 55
                1. Environment . . . . . . . . . . . . . . . . . . . . . . . . . . . . . . . . . 55
                2. Range. . . . . . . . . . . . . . . . . . . . . . . . . . . . . . . . . . . . . . . 56
                3. Position . . . . . . . . . . . . . . . . . . . . . . . . . . . . . . . . . . . . . 56
                   a. Foot and Hand Positions . . . . . . . . . . . . . . . . . . . . . 57
                4. Stances. . . . . . . . . . . . . . . . . . . . . . . . . . . . . . . . . . . . . . 59
                5. Maneuvers. . . . . . . . . . . . . . . . . . . . . . . . . . . . . . . . . . . 59
                6. Targets. . . . . . . . . . . . . . . . . . . . . . . . . . . . . . . . . . . . . . 60
                7. Zone Theories . . . . . . . . . . . . . . . . . . . . . . . . . . . . . . . . 60
                8. Natural Weapons. . . . . . . . . . . . . . . . . . . . . . . . . . . . . . 61
                9. Natural Defenses . . . . . . . . . . . . . . . . . . . . . . . . . . . . . . 62
                10. Breathing . . . . . . . . . . . . . . . . . . . . . . . . . . . . . . . . . . . 62
                11. Tailoring. . . . . . . . . . . . . . . . . . . . . . . . . . . . . . . . . . . . 63
                12. Physical and Mental Conditioning. . . . . . . . . . . . . . . 65
CHAPTER 5 -- NATURE OF THE ATTACK . . . . . . . . . . . . . . . . . . . . . 67
                1. Web of Knowledge . . . . . . . . . . . . . . . . . . . . . . . . . . . . 68
                2. How to Read the Web of Knowledge. . . . . . . . . . . . . 70
                3. Web of Knowledge for Belt Requirements . . . . . . . . 71
CHAPTER 6 -- AN ANALYTICAL STUDY OF MOTION. . . . . . . . . . . 89
                1. Organizational Chart on Motion. . . . . . . . . . . . . . . . 94
CHAPTER 7 -- DETERMINING YOUR CHOICE OF ACTION . . . . . . 97
CHAPTER 8 -- SELF-DEFENSE TECHNIQUES. . . . . . . . . . . . . . . . . . . 101
                1. Benefits and Pointers. . . . . . . . . . . . . . . . . . . . . . . . . . 102
                2. Reinforcing Ingredients . . . . . . . . . . . . . . . . . . . . . . . 104
                   a. Speed . . . . . . . . . . . . . . . . . . . . . . . . . . . . . . . . . . . . 104
                   b. Power. . . . . . . . . . . . . . . . . . . . . . . . . . . . . . . . . . . . 105
                3. Selected Techniques . . . . . . . . . . . . . . . . . . . . . . . . . . 106

CHAPTER    9 -- FREESTYLE (SPARRING) ........................ 191
                1. Acceptance. ................................ 192
                2. Environment .............................. 192
                3. Range .................................... 195
                a. Dimensional Stages of Action ............... 195
                4. Position ................................. 196
                a. Positioned Blocks. ........................ 197
                b. Zone Theories ........................... 198
                c. Reactionary Postures and Positions ........... 198
                5. Maneuvers ............................... 198
                a. Foot Maneuvers. ......................... 199
                b. Body Maneuvers ......................... 199
                c. Feinting. ................................ 199
                6. Targets .................................. 200
                a. Postures and Positions in
                   Relation to Targets. ....................... 201
                b. Contouring Principle ...................... 202
                   1) Complementary Angle ................... 202
                c. Angle of Incidence. ....................... 202
                d. Surface Concentration. ..................... 202
                e. Penetration. ............................. 203
                7. Natural Weapons. ......................... 203
                a. Strikes. ................................. 203
                8. Natural Defenses .......................... 204
                a. Blocks. ................................. 204
                9. Mental and Physical Constituents .............. 204
                a. A Review of Contributing Factors. ............ 205
                10. Freestyle Techniques. ...................... 205
                11. Explanation of Freestyle Techniques. .......... 208
                12. Notes on Freestyle Techniques ............... 230
CHAPTER    10 -- CONCLUSION. .............................. 233
SUCCESS. ..................................................... 234
GLOSSARY OF TERMINOLOGY ................................. ix

# ACKNOWLEDGEMENTS

My thanks go to those whose help made this volume possible. The list of names get longer with each volume. My gratitude is extended to my son, Ed Jr., whose typesetting and layout knowledge has made each publication easier to complete, in addition to his graphic artistic talents. My indebtedness and appreciation also goes to Jim Grunwald whose patience, suggestions, innovations, and creative photography never cease to amaze me. Editing and proofreading was painstakingly done by my wife, Leilani, Arnold Inouye, Skip Hancock, and David Sites. Models who posed for the photos were Frank Trejo, Ron Chapel, Howard Silva, Barbara Hale, Dennis Conatser, and Tommy Chavez. Photos of Leē Wedlake, Jr. were utilized to illustrate the Forms in Chapter 3. Additional thanks also go to Lee for writing the preface for Volume 3. Extracts from Tom Riskas' thesis were very helpful in specific areas of this volume. And last, but not least, I extend my appreciation to W. Craig McCoy for writing the preface for this volume and to my daughter, Sheri for helping with the photo layout.

# DEDICATION

To all readers of my five volume series of *Infinite Insights into Kenpo*, who, with an open mind, have taken on the challenge to examine, investigate, explore, expand, and expound on the principles, and concepts offered therein, I dedicate this book.

# PLEDGE

**BLACK BELT PLEDGE** - I hold that my time and my skill are the assets of my profession, assets which grow in value as I progress in the Art until, as a Third Degree Black Belt, I stand as a fully qualified instructor. It shall also be my responsibility to protect any student from ravenous individuals who would try to take advantage of personal weaknesses to divest the gullible into unprofitable paths, to preserve the sacred things, God, family, country, and Association, I pledge my all.

# ABOUT THE PLEDGE

This pledge is also an extension of the Creed, composed and designed to further promulgate spiritual character and judgement among the Black Belt Ranks. As extensions, they, too, denote the Martial Artist's way of life in today's environment and, therefore, also act as a regulatory guide to aid the Martial Artist in developing sensitivity, awareness, discernment, receptiveness, understanding, leniency, tolerance, compassion, and a keen sense of justice.

# PREFACE

All living things inevitably fight for their lives. The Human Race is no exception to this rule. From conception, to birth, to the last breath, we fight for the right to live. We fight for jobs, knowledge, shelter, mates, and space to raise our children. Even to this very day, we fight against our own species to survive.

Because of worldwide aggression the need to study or develop methods of self-defense becomes more essential daily. Those who are not concerned, often become statistics. Many of them have been buried without even a monument to commemorate their passing, or mark the grave where they lie.

To fill this need, practical methods of training our minds and bodies in self-defense have been adopted and borrowed from a number of sources. In the last 80 years a number of training systems, known collectively as the Asian martial arts, have been transferred to the Western world and incorporated with our indigenous fighting methods. However, along with these borrowed training methods have come customs, attitudes, beliefs and a vocabulary (language) common to the cultures in which they originated, but not necessarily compatible with those countries adopting them.

Language can be a barrier. For knowledge to be understood, it must be transmitted in a language compatible with the customs, attitudes, beliefs, and terms of the people who seek that knowledge. It must be further emphasized, that while an interpreter is needed, learning goes beyond the language barrier. Not only does the learner need an interpreter who can communicate this amalgam of ideas and motion in its new home, but one who can correctly translate the exact concepts and principles underlying each basic motion. Obviously, what is needed is a teacher as well as an interpreter. Unfortunately, great teachers are rare. There are more great practitioners of the art than there are great teachers. The reason for this is simple, while mastering an art requires both knowing and doing, communicating an art so that others may also know and do is far more difficult. A great teacher, therefore, is not only one who is a great practitioner, but one who can effectively convey his knowledge as well.

Ed Parker is such a teacher. Known for his physical ability and innovative fighting concepts, he is an effective conveyor of Martial Arts knowledge. This book is the fifth in a series of five volumes that reveals the secrets of his prowess, as a Martial Artist. Described in magazines as the *"magician of motion"*, Ed Parker succeeded in the marriage of both the Asian training systems, and those native to the Western world -- thus emerged an eclectic self-defense system greater than its origins. Innovative in its concepts and actions, and using a language that is suitable to our time and place, he has made *his system of Kenpo* compatible with the customs, beliefs and attitudes of our present day *American environment.*

This book, Volume 5, is a series of educational tests designed for the serious student. Using easily understood terms that are harmonious with the Western world, they provide a guide to the methods and concepts in this volume, as well as the four preceding volumes, and will unquestionably help you to become a more skilled practitioner of the Martial Arts.

**W. Craig McCoy**
6th Degree Black

# CHAPTER 1
# INTRODUCTION

The main purpose of writing Volume V is to incorporate all of the basic theories, concepts, and principles discussed in Volumes I through IV to achieve a more complete understanding of how these mental and physical aspects relate, function, and apply. Acquiring this knowledge not only develops refined techniques, but can result in success in combat.

Combat without preparation can prove disastrous to say the least. *Realistic* preparations, therefore, must be made to overcome environmental conditions, unpredictable events, or to curtail an opponent whose unorthodox actions and reactions can unexpectedly create variables that may cause defeat. Realizing that an attack can dictate and direct your defense necessitates learning combat in total. This involves learning the basic movement patterns found in forms (Katas), self-defense and sparring techniques (freestyle for both tournament and street) to a point of total familiarity and instinctive reaction. As your natural reflexes develop spontaneous reaction, movements become reflexive with maximum certainty.

Teaching the total concept of applying Kenpo is difficult since teaching also entails learning. The teacher as well as the student must be able to communicate. The question then is how do you properly communicate? How do you bridge the learning and teaching gap? Years of teaching has taught me to effectively bridge the learning and teaching gap through the use of *analogies*, *short stories*, and *sayings* (quotes). Since learning depends heavily upon the manner in which a subject is conveyed, I have had a measure of success because I have related facts with personal experience. In actuality, this process of relating fact to experience can aid everyone who seeks knowledge in various fields of endeavor. Communication, therefore, becomes effective when facts or concepts surrounding a given situation can be paralleled to past experiences. When a student can equate and relate his past experiences with what he is presently absorbing, learning becomes easy. Parallel the concepts of a new subject, technique, or experience and you will unquestionably quicken the learning process.

The Chinese symbolically related their fighting techniques to the movements of various animals. Because of China's vast size, the populace imitated the movements of specific animals (the deer, tiger, bear, monkey), reptiles and fowl of all types which were indigenous to their region. Thus, they created many systems of Martial Arts. Since we are seldom exposed to these animals in their natural habitat, attempts to observe and imitate their methods of fighting are difficult. Then too, how practical are these moves in today's environment? A limited amount of mimicking movements may work, but an entire system based on these movements would be impractical.

The deer had been chosen to imitate its sure-footedness, quickness and swift movements.

The tiger for its strength, ferocity and powerful dynamic movements.

The bear could have been considered for its stance, strength and bravery.

The monkey for its wit, cunningness, flexibility and ability to imitate almost everything that a human can do.

I have bridged the learning and teaching gap by paralleling the principles and concepts of our language (written and spoken), numeric system, and music system to those of the Martial Arts. These analogies are remarkably similar in context and are common to nearly everyone, therefore, they quicken most student's comprehension. I recommend that all instructors use analogies as tools in bringing details into proper perspective. Providing that an instructor has a comprehensive knowledge of many concepts and principles of combat, it is his duty to convey this knowledge to his student. Only effective communication can ultimately lend itself to the appropriate usage of such concepts and principles of combat.

In retrospect, training can be successfully accomplished, in part, if a student first seeks knowledge from an instructor who fully realizes the true essence of the various concepts and principles involved in combat. Secondly, the student further owes it to himself to not only ask what concepts and principles are involved in a technique (self-defense or sparring), but upon what conceptual basis each technique rests. Realizing the true essence of the movements in a technique, the student should then be made to realize that although techniques are first taught to follow a predetermined pattern of movements, they are still to be looked upon as flexible ideas. Techniques, therefore, are not to be executed as predetermined movements, but viewed as ideas that can be altered during combat to suit the situation.

Every student needs a strong basis of ideas founded upon *realistic* concepts and principles. Implanting various ideas in the form of situational techniques teaches a student to conceptualize these ideas as random references that can be activated spontaneously. However, the worth of these ideas is contingent upon the student's ability to absorb, comprehend, express, alter, exchange, and apply them in combat. While all combinations of movements broaden the base of our alternatives, they, nevertheless, depend upon the student's ability to function, and properly apply his ideas during combat. Thus, through the acquisition of alternatives, individuality and flexibility are destined to develop -- becoming dominant defensive tools in preparing for combat.

While students are encouraged to view techniques (self-defense or sparring) as ideas that can be altered instantly, being aware of a number of types of reactions stemming from an unpredictable opponent is another concept of technique training. Excluding emotional involvement, awareness can act as a prelude to instinctive and spontaneous reaction. Awareness, however, does not always provide you with the ability to predict what your opponent's reactions will be. It rather triggers your instinctive reactions without thinking of what is, or should be. Sequential preferences, therefore, are not thought of, they just happen. Thus, your ability to alter, expand, reduce, substitute, control, or change a technique is not a thinking function. It is one of feel and instinct.

As mentioned in Volume I, Chapter Six, it is when you reach the *Spontaneous Stage* that natural weapons function as if they had a mind of their own. Here again, this is the stage where a technique is not thought of at the moment of action. Instead, your actions and reactions are automatically activated and harmoniously blend with the encounter. You do not think. Your natural weapons think for themselves; they operate independent of your thinking process.

Ultimate flexibility, then, is the ability to alter, expand reduce, substitute, control, or change from one sequence of movements to another without having to think. Your response is instinctive when it is triggered by a given stimuli. The mind does not question what has to be done, it instinctively supplies you with answers that work. Thus, a technique is not intended to be thought of on the street, or executed as predetermined.

As responses become instinctive, you soon learn to react from all body positions *(points of origin)*. Your natural weapons do not cock, they instinctively respond from wherever they are located at the time of combat. Even clothing or objects you may have with you at the time of combat should pose no threat to your response. Kicks are activated despite the certainty that your pants will tear. Dignity, embarrassment, shame, humiliation, or disgrace are not even considered. Instinctive training eliminates such mental distractions, especially during a life and death situation.

Being able to instinctively react from all body positions *(points of origin)* reciprocally teaches you how to function from varying distances. You learn what natural weapon is most effective from close medium, or long range distances. If you are out of range, you learn to instinctively close the gap (through your use of *maneuvers*) to obtain a strategic position. You soon realize that it is the time that a natural weapon takes to reach its target plus the effect it produces that determines victory or defeat. Being totally familiar with your basics causes timing to become precise, range to be calculated automatically, and the choice of natural weapons (hands or feet) instinctively determined with each given situation.

It must be emphasized, however, that your reaction (or action) must be gauged proportionately with the speed of your opponent's action (or reaction). If your opponent's action is slow gauge your reaction accordingly. Should your opponent's speed concern you, *beat his action by meeting it.* Going with your opponent's action lessens the chance of your success. Meeting your opponent's action is one of two methods by which your reaction can beat his action. The second method is to have the target move out of the way first.

**To beat action, meet it.**

4

There are other factors that determine the success of your reaction (or action), (1) the location of your opponent's target areas in terms of height, width, and depth zones, (2) the accessibility of your opponent's targets resulting from his posture (defensive or otherwise), (3) the location of your natural weapons in terms of your posture, and as already pointed out, (4) the distance or range that exists between targets on your opponent's body and your natural weapons.

Subsequently, you must not lose sight of your opponent's reaction time. While attacking a specific target, contemplate the time it will take for your opponent to react. It stands to reason that if your opponent does not react quickly or have enough time to successfully block your strike, victory can be yours. It is, therefore, to your benefit to frequently select targets that take time to protect. Limbs used as defensive blockades should also be viewed as prime targets. Breakdown your opponent's defense and you will be free to select and hit targets which are more critical.

It goes without saying that an unexpected attack does not allow you time to stretch or loosen your muscles. This can be a concern since balance is not effectively maintained by cold muscles. At this point, you must employ all the knowledge you have acquired to your utmost ability. Limited knowledge that has been mastered can be effective despite the fact that your muscles may be cold. It is the skill with which you employ these mastered moves that makes the difference. Although power should be included with your skill, do not think about the power you are rendering only, but also about the punishment that your opponent can withstand as well.

While speed often enhances power, it is not the root of power. Maximum power comes from all of the elements of focus -- torque (rotating force), body momentum (where body and foot maneuvers are in "sync" with the action of your natural weapons), gravitational marriage (where the dropping of your body weight becomes an asset), proper body alignment, penetration and the ability to harmoniously combine these elements with breath control and the superconscious mind. Even greater power can be generated if you combine your striking action with the force of your opponent's action. To borrow your opponent's force is to gain a distinct advantage and thereby increase the power of your action.

A standing Kenpo philosophy is to avoid giving an opponent knowledge of your most effective weapons and favorite targets. You are to keep them in reserve for a time when your opponent least expects to be attacked by them. However, if his target areas are invitingly exposed do not hesitate to attack them.

To summarize, Volume V is a culmination of all aspects of combat discussed in Volumes I to IV. It deals with the application of mental and physical strategy in bringing about combat balance. Included in this balance are environmental perception and responsiveness -- which add up to combat victory.

Exceptional emphasis is placed on concepts and principles. As your experience, knowledge, and understanding of principles increases, you will discover, as I have, that they become technical tools that refine your movements. *Technical refinement* is the key that elevates you from a *salesman of motion*, to a *mechanic of motion*, and finally to an *engineer of motion*. You will also learn that an in-depth study of these concepts and principles will also make you aware of the importance of **TAILORING** concepts and principles to the needs of individuals.

I cannot overemphasize the value of concepts and principles. When one principle is applied, it will chronologically trigger another. When this chain reaction of concepts and principles occurs, it not only adds to the continuous flow of uninterrupted action, but residually helps to maximize all of your efforts.

The *self-defense techniques* in this volume are dissected anatomically to increase your understanding of some of the principles that exist within each step that comprise a technique. Thus, the more you become acquainted with these concepts and principles, the more apparent they become in the steps of a technique. When this level is achieved, you will become a *technician of motion* capable of reacting instinctively and spontaneously in every instance. The *formulation* steps discussed in this volume teach you how to progressively structure your *freestyle techniques* to a point of spontaneous reaction. Accomplish this response and you will inevitably refine your combat skills.

# CHAPTER 2
# IMPORTANCE OF BASICS

There are many who can speak a language, but are unable to either read or write it. Likewise, there are many who fight, but have never really learned how to fight effectively. To be competent, efficient and effective with any language or fighting skill, you must learn to logically and realistically *structure your basics*. The basics of English, our written and spoken language, stem from the proper use of the twenty six letters found in the alphabet. Our vocabulary depends on how we combine these letters to form words. As the number of words we master increases so does our vocabulary. Competent training in Kenpo begins and ends with basics. It would be faulty to assume that once we learn the basics we should go no further. Consequently, basics should be taught from the *embryonic stage* to the *sophisticated stage*. Beginning students should first learn to structure basic moves as they structure words. In doing so, care should be taken to arrange the sequence of movements sensibly so that they correctly *spell* the desired pattern of motion. Each move learned, whether it is used defensively or offensively, should be viewed as an *"alphabet of motion"* which, when combined with other moves, forms *"words and sentences of motion"* that make sense. Pushing the analogy a bit further we can say that whether we are striving to understand the structure of a sentence, or that of a self-defense technique we must first acquaint ourselves with the rules and formulas that insure their effectiveness.

Pronouncing a word through the process of *phonetics* is the next step after learning to spell. Likewise, through a process of *"physical phonetics"* moves can be taught syllabically. An entire move can be pronounced by accenting each step -- a *"by-the-number"* stage, so to speak. Once a student becomes familiar with the move, accented syllables are then accelerated and refined as the move becomes more fluid.

The third step, after spelling and pronouncing a move, requires *defining* it. *Definition* is essential if we wish to understand the meaning, capabilities, and limitations of each move. Any restriction to fully understanding the meaning or meanings of a move limits the scope of its usefulness. As beginning students

7

learn to apply embryonic basics, they soon learn that a single move may take on several meanings; that is, instead of a move accomplishing a single purpose, a number of functions may be performed in a single action. When this happens, embryonic moves transcend to sophistication.

The final stage in this analogy is the structuring of our defined moves into meaningful statements or movement patterns. Just as we need to know how to structure words within a sentence, so must we be able to know how to structure moves within a movement pattern. Techniques are created by the assemblage of sensible movement patterns. Such patterns in their extended versions form *"sentences and paragraphs of motion."* As we further strive to understand the structure of a technique, we become aware of the rules that we must apply to insure logical order. Thus, we are able to view each technique as though it had a *subject* (represented by the *defender*), a *predicate* (referring to the *action and reaction that occurs*) and an *object* (represented by the *opponent*). The *subject becomes the weapon*, the *predicate the method of execution*, and the *object the target(s)*.

The following listing by Tom Riskas further parallels the many facets of our written language and the similar ingredients needed to emerge victorious in combat.

## WRITING RULES

1. Check to see that all sentences are in the most logical or effective order.
2. Make sure that each modifier (adjective or adverb) contributes to the precise meaning of the sentence.
3. Be sure you effectively place a supporting clause.
4. Simplify clauses or phrases.
5. Cluster a few key words to simplify long descriptive sentences.
6. Make sure that the subject, predicate and possessive pronouns agree.
7. Check passive sentences to see if they should be made active.

## FIGHTING RULES

1. Strategically plan your movements to effectively handle the task at hand.
2. Don't embellish a technique with showy, unnecessary moves.
3. Support your primary moves with checks and secondary follow-up moves.
4. Don't waste your movements. Sophisticate, don't complicate.
5. Employ economy of motion. Combine and sophisticate your moves.
6. Don't move out of context with your opponent. Relate your reaction to his action.
7. Eliminate passive movements. They are a waste of time and energy.

8. Don't use any unnecessary words.

8. Simplify -- be direct and efficient.

9. Be as positive and definite as possible.

9. Be aggressive and assertive. Impose your strength on your opponent. Employ positive thinking.

10. Handle all the details consistently and accurately.

10. Always check and follow-up. Don't overlook the discreet actions/reactions of your opponent. Be concerned with details.

You don't need to be an expert in English to understand the above correlation. However, while this relationship can be utilized to bring details into proper perspective, you must keep in mind that technique formation and the application of **SELF-DEFENSE** or **SPARRING TECHNIQUES** should be based on tangible as well as logical concepts. "When one knows his subject, fear of verbally answering is not a problem. Fear may come about if one has to physically express himself."

# CHAPTER 3
# BASICS IN MOTION

This chapter deals with **BASICS IN MOTION** -- moves that you have already learned to apply singularly (both defensive and offensive) choreographed into a series of moves that flow with precisioned continuity. As mentioned in Volume I, dance like routines incorporating defensive and offensive basic moves are called *Katas*, *Sets*, or *Forms* (terms vary with each country). They teach you to flow easily into changes of direction or angle. Primarily devised for home training, the dance is an encyclopedia of movements which can be used in a variety of situations. (The shorter forms in Kenpo are looked upon as being "dictionaries of movement".) It is a means for indexing basic movements as workable prearranged self-defense combinations. Usually practiced without a partner, the practitioner goes through his dance while visualizing imaginary opponents as he victoriously defeats them. However, as previously indicated, to learn a **FORM** without knowing its true meaning or intent is like learning how to spell or pronounce a word without ever learning its definition. If a **FORM** is practiced in this manner, how can proper emphasis be placed where it belongs? When teaching a **FORM**, explanation of its meaning and usefulness should be included so that the individual learning will know the exact purpose or purposes for which it was intended. Knowing the purpose for doing it makes it possible for the student to place proper emphasis at the right moment. Knowing where to place the emphasis will give the **FORM** greater meaning. As a result, perfection of the **FORM** can be *assured*.

Since most of our beginning Kenpo **FORMS** are skeletal structures of **SELF-DEFENSE TECHNIQUES**, I feel that it is necessary that we discuss, and study a few Forms required in Kenpo. As you become acquainted with the **FORMS** pictorially demonstrated in this chapter, please note how they actually form, or mold the basic elements of a **SELF-DEFENSE TECHNIQUE**. Consequently, the primary elements of **SELF-DEFENSE TECHNIQUES** are encompassed in **FORMS**. Therefore, to learn a **FORM** is a preliminary stage to learning **SELF-DEFENSE TECHNIQUES**.

In addition, study will make you aware that although **FORMS** are dance-like routines incorporating a series of **SELF-DEFENSE TECHNIQUES**, they just touch on the major ingredients of a technique, where more often than not, the moves and angles necessary for effectiveness are disguised to purposely lead onlookers astray. Stated a little differently, many systems purposely disguise *their* **FORMS** to prevent onlookers from discovering what the **SELF-DEFENSE TECHNIQUES** truly contain.

The value of learning basics via **FORMS**, and **SELF-DEFENSE TECH-NIQUES** that residually result from those **FORMS**, cannot be over-emphasized. Multiple attacks prevalent on today's streets can be more effectively handled when you are fortified with this added knowledge. As you practice the following Kenpo **FORMS**, do them on an even surface first. Once you have become proficient, work them on uneven terrain. It goes without saying that you must study the elements contained within the **FORMS** and what you are to learn from them before undertaking the more advanced versions.

Hopefully, my approach to learning **FORMS** will be more meaningful because it will emphasize what each **FORM** contains and what you should learn from them. Motion without meaning serves no purpose. Therefore, as you learn the following **FORMS**, be sure to study the reasons for their creation. May you be successful in your efforts to learn these **FORMS**.

**NOTE:** Study, as well as practice, the **FORMS** before exploring the disciplines contained in **SELF-DEFENSE TECHNIQUES**. It is important that the parallels that exist between **FORMS**, and structured, or formulated **FREESTYLE TECHNIQUES** also be incorporated.

The following Kenpo forms were selected for your home study. It was my original intention to illustrate them using Lee Wedlake, Jr. as a model several years ago. As I viewed the photos of Lee, I felt that there were too many distractions (the black gi, distorted shades of gray, designs on the patch, etc.) that diverted one's attention from truly benefiting from their training. While it is true that "a photo is worth a thousand words", my son, Edmund, Jr., who is a graphic artist by profession, convinced me that, in this case, illustrated drawings would be better than photos. As I viewed my son's drawings, I could see that clarity was more apparent. Distractions were, indeed, minimized and a broader understanding achieved. Lee Wedlake, Jr.'s efforts, however, were not futile. It was his photos that my son used as models to complete the drawings.

Illustrated drawings have produced residual benefits. Drawings can be more compactly placed on a page without loss of clarity. As an educational aid to enhance your understanding of the forms, my son has added *horizontal lines* to give the *illusion of actual movement*. This technique makes it possible for you to perceive height, depth, and width, as well as give you a better sense of direction when you are practicing your forms. Arrows have also been added to help you become aware of follow-up moves. Only those arrows which are pertinent have been included.

Another educational aid has been the use of alphabets and letters. Letters have been primarily used for the beginning and ending of a salutation, and numbers used to describe the form itself. In some of the illustrations, you will find an illustration has both an alphabet and letter. Although these instances are rare, they are significant as you will see in the copies describing the illustrations.

# SHORT FORM 1

   **Short Form 1** was developed to teach a beginner how to retreat from an opponent while taking advantage of the free space around him. Environmental consideration is important because it determines what one can or cannot do. In **Short Form 1**, it is assumed that environment favors the practitioner who is allowed freedom to move about. The following information should apprise you of what the form *contains and is teaching you* to enhance your understanding of **Short Form 1** and why it was created:

**It Contains:**
   1. Moves that are strictly defensive.
   2. Stances:
      a. Attention
      b. Horse
      c. Neutral
   3. Basic blocks:
      a. Inward
      b. Outward
      c. Upward
      d. Downward
   4. Double blocks (Double Factor):
      a. High
      b. Low
   5. Four basic angles of attack.
   6. Back elbow strike while blocking.
   7. Nineteen moves including both sides and up close.

**It Teaches:**
   1. Staying down while in a stance.
   2. To use an erect carriage.
   3. Increasing peripheral vision.
   4. Always looking at your opponent.
   5. Never exposing your back unnecessarily.
   6. How to cover in a neutral bow stance.
   7. To keep your head at a constant level while changing stances.
   8. How to retreat from an opponent when you turn to face then unknown.
   9. Basic timing of hands and feet.
   10. How to block while retreating. (Opposite hand, opposite foot.)
   11. Relaxing and tensing at the proper moment.
   12. Angle changes in preparation for a mass attack.
   13. How to use the opposite arm as a hidden weapon.
   14. How to move up and down in an "L" pattern.
   15. Repetition of the four basic blocks while you are retreating.
   16. To have your block make contact at a distance from you so that your opponent's punch will be diverted.
   17. Crisp moves with snap and torque.

# SALUTATION

All Kenpo forms commence and end with a salutation. In **Short Form 1,** the **salutation** begins with **(a)** the **attention stance, (b) bowing** your head, and **(c)** moving your left foot to your left (to 3 o'clock) as you drop into a **horse stance,** while simultaneously placing your **left open hand over your right clenched fist.** Have your head **bow** to form a **(d) meditating horse stance.** (You are to clear your mind of all negative and irrelevant thoughts prior to commencing your form.) After a brief period of meditation (3 to 5 seconds), raise both of your hands **(e) above your head** and **(f)** smartly **drop them along the side of your thighs,** while simultaneously **closing your left foot to your right** to again form an **attention stance.** Illustrations **(g)** and **(h)** are the methods used to **signify** the form that you are about to demonstrate. **Half a finger** placed in the open palm of your opposite hand indicates two significant points, (1) that it is a **short** form, and (2) that the display of **one** finger reveals that it is **number one (#1)** of the **Short Form** series. Two or three half fingers placed in the palm **signifies** Short Form 2, or 3 respectively. Placing your finger or fingers in the right palm **signifies** that you will be demonstrating the **right side only.** When both palms are used, such as in the form shown, it **signifies** that you will be doing your form on **both the right and left sides.**

After **signifying** the form, execute a **(i) right front crossover** (toward 12 o'clock) **with your left open hand over your right clenched fist.** Have your **(j) left foot step forward** (left step through) **into a left 45 degree cat stance as you push both of your hands forward** (left open hand over right clenched fist) so that they are in line with, and on the same level as, your chin. **(k) Step back with your left foot with both of your hands opened and placed back-to-back. (l) Slide your right foot back into a right cat stance** as you **clench both fists** in preparation to cocking them to your hips. **(m) Shift your right foot alongside of your left foot (attention stance) as you cock both hands** (clenched and facing up) **to the sides of your waist. (n) Slide your left foot to the left** as you drop into a **training horse while simultaneously raising both of your hands above your head. Have the thumbs and fingers touch so that a triangle is formed between them. (o) Drop both hands** to chin level with your left open hand over your right clenched fist. **(p) Have the palms of both of your hands meet (as if praying),** and lower them to solar plexus level. **(q) Convert your praying hands to meditation hands** (left open hand over right clenched fist) as you bow your head in meditation. You are now ready to begin **Short Form 1.**

# START OF SHORT FORM 1

1. From your horse stance...

2. Have your left foot drop back toward 6:00 o'clock into a right neutral bow stance (facing 12:00), while executing a right inward block, simultaneous **"with"** a left back elbow strike.

3. Have your right foot drop back toward 6:00 into a left neutral bow stance (facing 12:00), while executing a left inward block, simultaneous **"with"** a right back elbow strike.

4. **Cover** (to your left) by moving your right foot toward 3:00 into a **transitory left neutral bow stance** (facing 9:00), while executing a **transitory right inward block,** simultaneous **"with"** a left back elbow strike **(a transitory move in preparation for the next block)**.

5. **Settle** into your left neutral bow stance (facing 9:00) while executing a left vertical outward block simultaneous **"with"** a right back elbow strike.

6. Have your left foot slide back as you form a **transitory left 45 degree cat stance** (facing 9:00), while executing a **transitory left inward block "with"** your right elbow remaining in place.

7. Continue to have your left foot travel back toward 3:00 as you **settle** into a right neutral bow (facing 9:00), while executing a right vertical outward block simultaneous **"with"** a left back elbow strike.

8. Cover (to your rear) by moving your right foot toward 9:00 into a **transitory left neutral bow** (facing 3:00), while executing a **transitory right inward block**), while your left elbow remains in place.

9. **Settle** into your left neutral bow stance (facing 3:00) while executing a left upward block simultaneous **"with"** a right back elbow strike.

# SHORT FORM 1 (continued)

10. Have your left foot slide back as you form a **transitory left 45 degree cat stance** (facing 3:00), while executing a **transitory left inward block "with"** your right elbow remaining in place.

11. Continue to have your left foot travel back toward 9:00 as you **settle** into a right neutral bow (facing 3:00), while executing a right upward block simultaneous **"with"** a left back elbow strike.

12. **Cover** (to your right) by moving your left foot toward 12:00 into a **transitory right neutral bow** (facing 6:00), while cocking your right arm horizontally across your waist (palm up) **"with"** the left arm slightly forward.

13. **Settle** into your right neutral bow stance (facing 6:00) while executing a right downward block, simultaneous **"with"** a left back elbow strike.

14. Have your right foot slide back as you form a **transitory right 45 degree cat stance** (facing 6:00), while executing a **transitory right inside downward block** (palm up), **"with"** your left arm cocked horizontally across your waist (palm up).

15. Continue to have your right foot travel back toward 12:00 as you **settle** into a left neutral bow (facing 6:00), while executing a left downward block simultaneous **"with"** a right back elbow strike.

16. Move your left foot clockwise into a horse stance (facing 12:00) **"with"** your left open hand placed on your right clenched fist.

**NOTE:** You may continue the left side of this form by doing the exact moves (illustrations 2 through 16) to the opposite side (mirror image of right side).

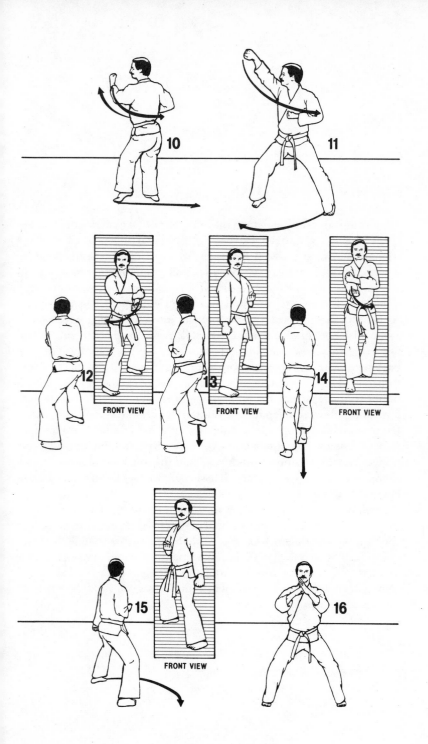

**10**

**11**

**12** FRONT VIEW

**13** FRONT VIEW

**14** FRONT VIEW

**15** FRONT VIEW

**16**

# CLOSING SALUTATION:

The **closing salutation** ends from the **horse stance (r)** by raising both of your hands **(s) above your head. Have the thumbs and fingers touch so that a triangle is formed between them. (t)** Smartly **drop** your hands along the side of your thighs, while simultaneously **closing your left foot to your right** to form an **attention stance.** Execute a **(u) right front crossover** (toward 12 o'clock) **with your left open hand over your right clenched fist.** Have your **(v) left foot step forward** (left step through) **into a left 45 degree cat stance** as you **push both of your hands forward** (left open hand over right clenched fist) so that they are in line with, and on the same level as, your chin. **(w) Step back with your left foot with both your hands opened and placed back-to-back. (x) Slide your right foot back into a right cat stance** as you **clench both fists** in preparation to cocking them to your hips. **(y) Shift your right foot alongside of your left foot (attention stance)** as you **cock both hands** (clenched and facing up) **to the sides of your waist. (z) Slide your left foot to the left** as you drop **into a training horse while simultaneously raising both of your hands above your head. Have the thumbs and fingers touch so that a triangle is again formed between them. (aa) Drop both hands to chin level** with your left open hand over your right clenched fist. **(bb) Have the palms of both of your hands meet (as if praying),** and lower them to solar plexus level. **(cc)** Again raise both of your hands **above your head with the thumbs and fingers touching so that they form a triangle between them. (dd)** Smartly **drop your hands along the side of your thighs,** while simultaneously **closing your left foot to your right** to form an **attention stance. (ee) Bow** your head. **(ff) Lift** your head as you end this form in an **attention stance.**

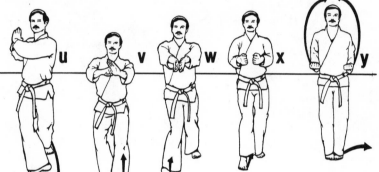

# LONG FORM 1

**Long Form 1** was developed to teach a beginner how to defend while retreating, before following-up with a strike. The moves in this form are simple. Checks to prevent retaliatory moves are not taught at this stage. This is done to eliminate confusion and not to cloud the mind of a beginner. This form again takes advantage of free space in addition to other facets of environment which favor the practitioner. The following information should apprise you of what the form *contains and is teaching you* to enhance your understanding of *Long Form 1* and why it was created:

**It Contains:**
1. Moves that are defensive.
2. Moves that are offensive.
3. Basic stances:
    a. Attention
    b. Horse
    c. Neutral Bow
    d. Forward Bow
    e. Cat
4. Basic blocks:
    a. Inward
    b. Outward
    c. Upward
    d. Downward
5. Additional blocks:
    a. Inside Downward Palm Down
    b. Inside Downward Palm Up
    c. Push Down
6. Punches:
    a. Straight Horizontal Thrust
    b. Uppercut
    c. Roundhouse
7. Directions which one can punch out of a horse stance while facing 12 o'clock:
    a. To 12 o'clock
    b. To 1:30 and 10:30
    c. To 3 o'clock and 9 o'clock
8. Strikes:
    a. Back Elbow Strike while blocking
    b. Back Elbow Strike while punching
    c. Outward Diagonal Elbow

9. Transitional Moves:
   a. Cat Stance
   b. Cover
10. Four basic angle changes
11. Two types of cover:
   a. While retreating
   b. While advancing
12. Double Factor: High and Low

**It Teaches:**
1. The elements that Short Form #1 teaches.
2. How to block while advancing, same hand - same foot.
3. How to block while stationary:
   a. Opposite hand - opposite foot.
   b. Same hand - same foot.
4. How to increase distance while covering.
5. How to decrease distance while covering.
6. How to block and counter, using different hands.
7. How to use opposing forces while punching.
8. How to use body rotation for power, while punching.
9. How to use the opposite arm as a hidden weapon:
   a. While blocking
   b. While punching
10. How to use transitional moves for power.
11. Basic timing of hands and feet:
   a. Defensive moves
   b. Offensive moves
12. Use of the Double Factor
13. How to use transitional moves offensively.
14. How to use transitional moves defensively.
15. How to use upper and lower case movements.
16. Proper angles when blocking off the rear hand.
17. How to use transitional moves while retreating.
18. How to use transitional moves while advancing.
19. How to block multiple attacks from a single opponent.
20. How to maintain constant head level while using transitional stances.
21. How to block below the waist, using the hands.
22. Angles, directions, and methods of execution when punching.
23. The importance of supporting and bracing a punch with your rear heel on the ground when pivoting from a neutral bow to a forward bow.
24. That the head operates like a gyro on a ship's compass.
25. The concept of *body fusion.*
26. The principle of *contouring* when punching.

# SALUTATION

In **Long Form 1**, the **salutation** begins with **(a)** the **attention stance, (b) bowing** your head, and **(c)** moving your left foot to your left (to 3 o'clock) as you drop into a **horse stance**, while simultaneously placing your **left open hand over your right clenched fist**. Have your head **bow** to form a **(d) meditating horse stance**. (You are to clear your mind of all negative and irrelevant thoughts prior to commencing your form.) After a brief period of meditation (3 to 5 seconds), raise both of your hands **(e) above your head** and **(f)** smartly **drop them along the side of your thighs**, while simultaneously **closing your left foot to your right** to again form an **attention stance**. Illustrations **(g)** and **(h)** are the methods used to **signify** the form that you are about to demonstrate. A **fully extended finger** placed in the open palm of your opposite hand indicates two significant points, (1) that it is a **long** form, and (2) that the display of **one** finger (fully extended) reveals that it is **number one (#1)** of the **Long Form** series. Two or three fully extended fingers placed in the palm **signifies** Long Form 2, or 3 respectively. Placing your full length finger or fingers in the right palm **signifies** that you will be demonstrating the **right side only**. When both palms are used, such as in the form shown, it **signifies** that you will be doing your form on **both the right and left sides**.

After **signifying** the form, execute a **(i) right front crossover** (toward 12 o'clock) **with your left open hand over your right clenched fist**. Have your **(j) left foot step forward** (left step through) **into a left 45 degree cat stance** as you **push both of your hands forward** (left open hand over right clenched fist) so that they are in line with, and on the same level as, your chin. **(k) Step back with your left foot with both of your hands opened and placed back-to-back. (l) Slide your right foot back into a right cat stance** as you clench both fists in preparation to cocking them to your hips. **(m) Shift your right foot alongside of your left foot** (attention stance) as you cock both hands (clenched and facing up) **to the sides of your waist. (n) Slide your left foot to the left** as you drop **into a training horse while simultaneously raising both of your hands above your head. Have the thumbs and fingers touch so that a triangle is formed between them. (o) Drop both hands to chin level** with your left open hand over your right clenched fist. **(p) Have the palms of both of your hands meet (as if praying)**, and lower them to solar plexus level. **(q) Convert your praying hands to meditation hands** (left open hand over right clenched fist) **as you bow your head in meditation**. You are now ready to begin.

25

# START OF LONG FORM 1

1. From your horse stance . . .

2. Have your left foot drop back toward 6 o'clock into a right neutral bow, facing 12:00, as you simultaneously execute a right inward block **"with"** a left back elbow strike.

3. Pivot into a right forward bow toward 12 o'clock as you execute a left straight punch toward 12 o'clock simultaneously **"with"** a right back elbow strike.

4. Have your right foot slide into a right transitional cat stance while executing a right thrusting inward block **"with"** a left back elbow strike.

5. Complete your right step through by having your right foot plant back toward 6 o'clock into a left neutral bow. As you settle into your left neutral bow simultaneously execute a left inward block **"with"** a right back elbow strike.

6. Pivot into a left forward bow toward 12 o'clock as you execute a right straight punch to 12 o'clock simultaneous **"with"** a left back elbow strike.

7. Cover (by moving your right foot toward 3:00) into a left transitory neutral bow stance facing 9:00, while simultaneously executing a right hammering inward block.

8. Settle into a left neutral bow facing 9:00, while simultaneously executing a left vertical outward block **"with"** a right back elbow strike.

9. Pivot into a left forward bow toward 9 o'clock as you execute a right straight punch to 9 o'clock simultaneous **"with"** a left back elbow strike.

10. Have your left foot commence to drop back toward 3:00 into a transitory cat stance facing 9:00, while simultaneously executing a left transitory vertical outward block **"with"** a right back elbow strike.lt

11. Have your left foot continue to drop back toward 3:00 into a right neutral bow facing 9:00, while simultaneously executing a right vertical outward block **"with"** a left back elbow strike.

12. Pivot into a right forward bow toward 9 o'clock as you execute a left straight punch to 9 o'clock simultaneous **"with"** a right back elbow strike.

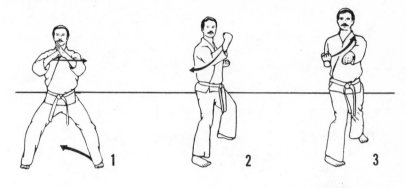

1   2   3

4   5   6

7   8   9

10   11   12

13. Cover (by having your right foot move toward 9:00), while delivering a left horizontal outward elbow strike.

14. Immediately pivot in-place into a left neutral bow facing 3:00, while simultaneously executing a left upward block "**with**" a right back elbow strike.

15. Pivot into a left forward bow toward 3 o'clock as you execute a right straight punch to 3 o'clock simultaneous "**with**" a left back elbow strike.

16. Have your left foot commence to drop back toward 9:00 into a left transitory cat stance facing 3:00, while simultaneously executing a left transitory thrusting inward block "**with**" a right back elbow strike.

17. Have your left foot continue to drop back toward 9:00 into a right neutral bow facing 3:00, while simultaneously executing a right upward block "**with**" a left back elbow strike.

18. Pivot into a right forward bow toward 3 o'clock as you execute a left straight punch to 3 o'clock simultaneous "**with**" a right back elbow strike.

19. Cover (this time the right foot steps out toward 6:00) into a right neutral bow facing 6:00, while simultaneously cocking (transitory move) your right arm horizontally across your body (palm up) as well as bringing your left arm slightly forward. (NOTE: Once this form has been suitably perfected convert your left arm into a left inside downward block (palm up) to act as an interim block.)

20. Immediately execute a right downward block "**with**" a left back elbow strike as you settle into your right neutral bow stance.

21. Pivot into a right forward bow toward 6 o'clock as you execute a left straight punch to 6 o'clock simultaneous "**with**" a right back elbow strike.

22. Have your right foot commence to drop back toward 12:00 into a right transitory cat stance facing 6:00, while simultaneously cocking (transitory move) your left arm horizontally across your body (palm up) as well as bringing your right arm slightly forward. (NOTE: Once this Form has been suitably perfected convert your right arm into a right inside downward block (palm up) to act as an interim block.)

23. Have your right foot continue to drop back toward 12:00 into a left neutral bow facing 6:00, while simultaneously executing a left downward block "**with**" a right back elbow strike.

24. Pivot into a left forward bow toward 6 o'clock as you execute a right straight punch to 6 o'clock simultaneous "**with**" a left back elbow strike.

**13**     **14**      **15**

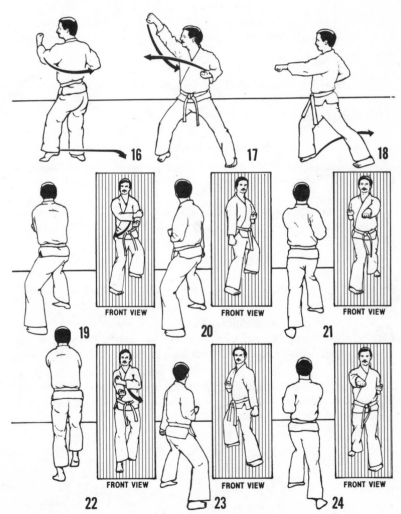

**16**     **17**     **18**

FRONT VIEW     FRONT VIEW     FRONT VIEW

**19**     **20**     **21**

FRONT VIEW     FRONT VIEW     FRONT VIEW

**22**     **23**     **24**

25. Pivot back into a left neutral bow facing 6:00, while simultaneously executing a left inward block **"with"** a right back elbow strike.

26. Execute a right inward block **"with"** a left back elbow strike.

27. Execute a left inward block **"with"** a right back elbow strike.

28. Your left foot steps back toward 12:00 into a right neutral bow facing 6:00, while simultaneously executing a right inward block **"with"** a left back elbow strike.

29. Execute a left inward block **"with"** a right back elbow strike.

30. Execute a right inward block **"with"** a left back elbow strike.

31. Cover (by moving your left foot toward 3:00) into a right neutral bow facing 9:00, while simultaneously executing a left transitory thrusting inward block **"with"** your right arm horizontally across your body (palm down).

32. Settle into your right neutral bow facing 9:00, while simultaneously executing a right vertical outward block **"with"** a left back elbow strike.

33. Execute a left vertical outward block **"with"** a right back elbow strike.

34. Execute a right vertical outward block **"with"** a left back elbow strike.

35. Have your right foot commence to drop back toward 3:00 into a right transitory cat stance facing 9:00, while simultaneously executing a right transitory hammering inward block with your left arm remaining in-place.

36. Have your right foot continue to drop back toward 3:00 as you settle into a left neutral bow facing 9:00, while simultaneously executing a left vertical outward block **"with"** a right back elbow strike.

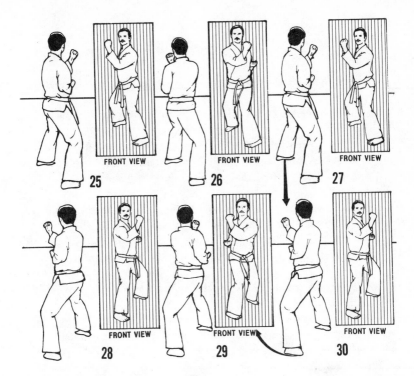

**25** FRONT VIEW    **26** FRONT VIEW    **27** FRONT VIEW

**28** FRONT VIEW    **29** FRONT VIEW    **30** FRONT VIEW

**31**    **32**    **33**

**34**    **35**    **36**

37. Execute a right vertical outward block "**with**" a left back elbow strike.

38. Execute a left vertical outward block "**with**" a right back elbow strike.

39. Cover (by moving your left foot toward 9:00) into a right neutral bow facing 3:00, while simultaneously executing a left transitory hammering inward block with your left arm remaining in-place.

40. Settle into your right neutral bow facing 3:00, while simultaneously executing a right upward block "**with**" a left back elbow strike.

41. Execute a left upward block "**with**" a right back elbow strike.

42. Execute a right upward block "**with**" a left back elbow strike.

43. Have your right foot commence to drop back toward 9:00 into a right transitory cat stance facing 3:00, while simultaneously executing a right transitory hammering inward block with your left arm horizontally across your body (palm up).

44. Your right foot drops back toward 9:00 into a left neutral bow facing 3:00, while simultaneously executing a left upward block "**with**" a right back elbow strike.

45. Execute a right upward block "**with**" a left back elbow strike.

46. Execute a left upward block "**with**" a right back elbow strike.

47. Cover (by moving your right foot toward 6:00) into a left neutral bow facing 12:00, while simultaneously cocking (transitory move) your left arm horizontally across your body (palm up) as well as bringing your right arm slightly forward. (NOTE: Once this Form has been suitably perfected convert your right arm into a right inside downward block (palm up) to act as an interim block.)

48. Settle into your left neutral bow facing 12:00, while simultaneously executing a left downward block "**with**" a right back elbow strike.

49. Execute a right downward block "**with**" a left back elbow strike.

50. Execute a left downward block "**with**" a right back elbow strike.

51. Have your left foot commence to drop back toward 6:00 into a into a transitory cat stance facing 12:00, while simultaneously cocking (transitory move) your right arm horizontally across your body (palm up) as well as bringing your left arm slightly back and horizontal to the ground (palm up). (NOTE: Once this form has been suitably perfected convert your left arm into a left inside downward block (palm up) to act as an interim block.)

52. Have your left foot continue to drop back toward 6:00 into a right neutral bow facing 12:00, while simultaneously executing a right downward block "**with**" a left back elbow strike.

53. Execute a left downward block "**with**" a right back elbow strike.

54. Execute a right downward block "**with**" a left back elbow strike.

**NOTE:** The remainder of this form constitutes moves that are isolated. They are not linked to produce logical working sequences, but are to be studied for their individual value.

55. Have your left foot move up (toward 9:00), and in line with your right foot, as you form a horse stance facing 12:00. Simultaneously execute a left inside downward block (palm down) "**with**" a right back elbow strike.

56. Execute a right inside downward block (palm down) simultaneously "**with**" a left back elbow strike.

57. Execute a left inside downward block (palm down) simultaneously "**with**" a right back elbow strike.

58. Execute a right inside downward block (palm up) simultaneously "**with**" a left back elbow strike.

59. Execute a left inside downward block (palm up) simultaneously "**with**" a right back elbow strike.

60. Execute a right inside downward block (palm up) simultaneously "**with**" a left back elbow strike.

49

50

51

52

53

54

55

56

57

58

59

60

61. Execute a left push-down block simultaneously **"with"** a right back elbow strike.

62. Execute a right push-down block simultaneously **"with"** a left back elbow strike.

63. Execute a left push-down block simultaneously **"with"** a right back elbow strike.

64. Execute a right straight thrust punch to 12 o'clock simultaneously **"with"** a left back elbow strike.

65. Execute a left straight thrust punch to 12 o'clock simultaneously **"with"** a right back elbow strike.

66. Execute a right straight thrust punch to 10:30 simultaneously **"with"** a left back elbow strike.

67. Execute a left straight thrust punch to 1:30 simultaneously **"with"** a right back elbow strike.

68. Execute a right straight thrust punch to 9 o'clock simultaneously **"with"** a left back elbow strike.

69. Execute a left straight thrust punch to 3 o'clock simultaneously **"with"** a right back elbow strike.

70. Execute a right uppercut punch to 12 o'clock simultaneously **"with"** a left back elbow strike.

71. Execute a left uppercut punch to 12 o'clock simultaneously **"with"** a right back elbow strike.

72. Have your left hand open in place as your right clenched fist meets the left open palm. **GO TO CLOSING SALUTATION.**

  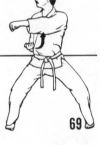

# CLOSING SALUTATION:

The **closing salutation** ends by raising both of your hands **(s) above your head. Have the thumbs and fingers touch so that a triangle is formed between them. (t)** Smartly **drop your hands along the side of your thighs,** while simultaneously **closing your left foot to your right** to form an **attention stance.** Execute a **(u) right front crossover** (toward 12 o'clock) **with your left open hand over your right clenched fist.** Have your **(v) left foot step forward** (left step through) **into a left 45 degree cat stance** as you **push both of your hands forward** (left open hand over right clenched fist) so that they are in line with, and on the same level as, your chin. **(w) Step back with your left foot with both your hands opened and placed back-to-back. (x) Slide your right foot back into a right cat stance** as you **clench both fists** in preparation to cocking them to your hips. **(y) Shift your right foot alongside of your left foot (attention stance)** as you **cock both hands** (clenched and facing up) **to the sides of your waist. (z) Slide your left foot to the left** as you drop **into a training horse while simultaneously raising both of your hands above your head. Have the thumbs and fingers touch so that a triangle is again formed between them. (aa) Drop both hands to chin level** with your left open hand over your right clenched fist. **(bb) Have the palms of both of your hands meet (as if praying),** and lower them to solar plexus level. **(cc) Again raise both of your hands above your head with the thumbs and fingers touching so that they form a triangle between them. (dd) Smartly drop your hands along the side of your thighs,** while simultaneously **closing your left foot to your right** to form an **attention stance. (ee) Bow** your head. **(ff)** Lift your head as you end this form in an **attention stance.**

# SHORT FORM 2

**Short Form 2** assumes an *environment* that restricts you from moving back. Therefore, the form was developed to teach a beginner how to defend while advancing. You can immediately strike after the block, or simultaneously block and strike. Although the moves in this form are simple, they do employ checks in anticipation of retaliatory moves. The form additionally introduces you to becoming coordinated with the periodic opening and closing of the fist. This is done intermittently through the course of your defensive and offensive moves. The following information should apprise you of what the form *contains and is teaching you* to enhance your understanding of *Short Form 2 and why it was created*:

## It Contains:

1. Basic Stances:
    a. Attention Stance
    b. Horse Stance
    c. Neutral Bow
    d. Cat Stance (transitory)
    e. Wide Rear Twist Stance
    f. Wide Kneel Stance
    g. Forward Bow
2. Basic Blocks:
    a. Inward
    b. Vertical outward
    c. Upward
    d. Downward
    e. Extended outward
3. 45° Degree Angle Changes
4. Natural Weapons:
    a. Handsword
    b. Fist {large knuckles}
    c. Middle knuckle fist
    d. Heel of palm
    e. Half-fist
5. Basic Methods of Execution:
    a. Thrusting
    b. Raking
    c. Snapping
6. Checking Strikes
7. Economy of Motion
8. Hard and Soft rythmatic timing
9. Simultaneous Defense with Offense

**It Teaches:**
1. How to defend yourself if backed up against a wall.
2. How to advance when defending.
3. How to use the opposite hand as a guard.
4. How to cover in a cat stance and then advance.
5. How to counter:
   a. Immediate strike after block.
   b. Simultaneous block and strike in the same direction.
   c. Simultaneous block and strike in the opposite directions.
6. How to shift from a neutral bow to a forward bow and the reverse.
7. How to step through with your action.
8. How to coordinate the clenching and the opening of your hand so you can readily alter your weapon as well as your target.
9. Marriage of Gravity while keeping an erect carriage.
10. How imperative it is to keep your thumb **IN** when executing a heel palm strike.
11. How to drop under a punch.
12. How to form and use the middle knuckle fist.
13. To get acquainted with the various methods of execution.
14. How to utilize the rear twist stance.
15. How to use circular movements with linear movements and vice-versa.
16. All eight angles of attack; 45° and 90° degree angles.
17. To step into the semi-unknown with a block as you counter.

# SALUTATION

In **Short Form 2,** the **salutation** begins with **(a)** the **attention stance, (b) bowing** your head, and **(c)** moving your left foot to your left (to 3 o'clock) as you drop into a **horse stance,** while simultaneously placing your **left open hand over your right clenched fist.** Have your head **bow** to form a **(d) meditating horse stance.** (You are to clear your mind of all negative and irrelevant thoughts prior to commencing your form.) After a brief period of meditation (3 to 5 seconds), raise both of your hands **(e) above your head** and **(f)** smartly **drop them along the side of your thighs,** while simultaneously **closing your left foot to your right** to again form an **attention stance.** Illustrations **(g)** and **(h)** are the methods used to **signify** the form that you are about to demonstrate. In this form **two half fingers** placed in the open palm of your opposite hand indicates two significant points, (1) that it is a **short** form, and (2) that the display of **two** fingers reveals that it is **number two (#2)** of the **Short Form** series. Three half fingers placed in the palm **signifies** Short Form 3. As stated previously your finger or fingers in the right palm **signifies** that you will be demonstrating the **right side only.** When both palms are used, such as in the form shown, it **signifies** that you will be doing your form on **both the right and left sides.**

After **signifying** the form, execute a **(i) right front crossover** (toward 12 o'clock) **with your left open hand over your right clenched fist.** Have your **(j) left foot step forward** (left step through) **into a left 45 degree cat stance** as you **push both of your hands forward** (left open hand over right clenched fist) so that they are in line with, and on the same level as, your chin. **(k) Step back with your left foot with both of your hands opened and placed back-to-back. (l) Slide your right foot back into a right cat stance** as you clench both fists in preparation to cocking them to your hips. **(m) Shift your right foot alongside of your left foot** (attention stance) as you cock both hands (clenched and facing up) **to the sides of your waist. (n) Slide your left foot to the left** as you drop **into a training horse while simultaneously raising both of your hands above your head. Have the thumbs and fingers touch so that a triangle is formed between them. (o) Drop both hands to chin level** with your left open hand over your right clenched fist. **(p) Have the palms of both of your hands meet (as if praying),** and lower them to solar plexus level. **(q) Convert your praying hands to meditation hands** (left open hand over right clenched fist) **as you bow your head in meditation.** You are now ready to begin.

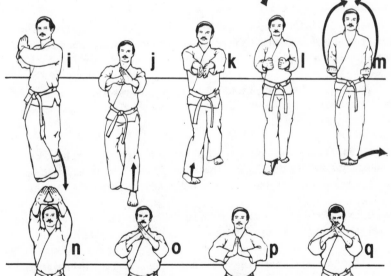

# START OF SHORT FORM 2

1. From your horse stance . . .

2. Have your right foot step forward toward 12 o'clock into a right neutral bow stance. Simultaneously deliver a right inward block, **"with"** your left hand checking at your solar plexus.

3. Execute a right outward handsword strike. (This is a diagonal chop delivered at neck level).

4. Have your left foot step forward toward 12 o'clock into a leftneutral bow stance, while simultaneously delivering a left inwardblock, **"with"** your right hand checking at your solar plexus.

5. Execute a left outward handsword strike. (This is a diagonal chop delivered at neck level).

6. Slide your left foot back and toward your right foot into a **transitory left 45 degree cat stance** and cock both fists at your right hip (right hand palm up and left hand palm down).

7. Have your left foot step toward 9 o'clock into a left neutralbow, while simultaneously delivering a left vertical outwardblock **"with"** a right straight thrust punch toward 9 o'clock. (This punch is at shoulder level.)

8. Slide your right foot toward your left foot into a **transitory right 45 degree cat stance** and cock both fists on the side ofyour left hip (left hand palm up and right hand palm down.

9. Have your right foot step toward 3 o'clock into a rightneutral bow, while simultaneously delivering a right verticaloutward block **"with"** a left straight thrust punch toward 3o'clock. (This punch is at shoulder level.)

10. Have your left foot step between 5 and 6 o'clock into a **transitory left wide kneel stance** and cock both fists along the side of your right chest.

11. Pivot counterclockwise **dropping** (under a punch that is delivered at head level) into a left wide kneel stance toward 6:00, while simultaneously delivering a left upward block, **"with"** a right vertical downward raking middle knuckle fist. (This is a downward hammering motion, making contact with the bottom side of the middle knuckle fist.)

SIDE VIEW

45

12. Have your right foot step between 12 and 1 o'clock into a transitory right wide kneel stance and cock both fists along the side of your left chest similar to step 10.

13. Pivot clockwise **dropping** (under a punch that is delivered at head level) into a right wide kneel stance toward 12:00, while simultaneously delivering a right upward block, **"with"** a left vertical downward raking middle knuckle fist. (This is a downward hammering motion, making contact with the bottom side of the middle knuckle fist.)

14. **Rotate your body counterclockwise** as you slide your left foot (counter-clockwise) toward 4:30 (between 4 and 5 o'clock) into a **transitory left cat stance.** Simultaneously execute a right inside downward block (palm up) as your left hand cocks to your right chest (palm up).

15. **Settle** into a left neutral bow stance (facing 4:30) while executing a left downward block simultaneous **"with"** a right back elbow strike. Your right hand is cocked (palm up) on your right hip.

16. Have your right foot **step through** toward 4:30 into a right neutral bow, while simultaneously delivering a right thrusting heel palm strike at face level, **"with"** a left horizontal forearm check at solar plexus level (under your right elbow).

17. **Rotate your body clockwise** as you slide your right foot (clockwise) toward 7:30 (between 7 and 8 o'clock) into a **transitory right cat stance.** Simultaneously execute a left inside downward block (palm up) as your right hand cocks at your left chest (palm up).

18. **Settle** into a right neutral bow stance (facing 7:30) while executing a right downward block simultaneous **"with"** a left back elbow strike. Your left hand is cocked (palm up) on your left hip.

19. Have your left foot **step through** toward 7:30 into a left neutral bow, while simultaneously delivering a left thrusting heel palm strike at face level, **"with"** a right horizontal forearm check at solar plexus level (under your left elbow).

**12**

**13**

**SIDE VIEW**

**14**

**15**

**16**

**17**

**18**

**19**

20. **Rotate your body counterclockwise** as you slide your right foot back toward your left foot to form a **transitory right 90 degree cat stance** facing 1:30 (between 1 and 2 o'clock). Simultaneously execute a left inward block as your right hand cocks horizontally across your waist (palm up).

21. Have your right foot **step forward** toward 1:30 into a right neutral bow. Simultaneously execute a right extended outward block, as you cock your left hand at the left side of your chest (palm up, half-fist).

22. Pivot into a right forward bow toward 1:30, while striking with a left snapping half-fist punch (palm down) at throat level. This is a transitory forward bow, so . . .

23. Immediately pivot back into a right neutral bow with your left half-fist snapping back to the left side of your chest.

24. Have your left foot slide toward your right foot and then as you turn counterclockwise with your upper body facing 10:30 (between 10 and 11 o'clock) continue to slide your right foot toward 10:30 into a transitory left 45 degree cat stance. Simultaneously execute a right inward block as your left hand cocks horizontally across your waist (palm up).

25. Have your left foot **step forward** toward 10:30 into a left neutral bow. Simultaneously execute a left extended outward block, as you cock your right hand at the right side of your chest (palm up, half-fist).

26. Pivot into a left forward bow toward 10:30, while strikingwith a right snapping half-fist punch (palm down) at throat level. This is a transitory forward bow, so . . .

27. Immediately pivot back into a left neutral bow with your right half-fist snapping back to the right side of your chest.

28. Bring your right foot up to and in line with your left foot to form a **meditating horse stance,** facing 12:00 **"with"** your left open hand placed on your right clenched fist. **GO TO CLOSING SALUTATION.**

# CLOSING SALUTATION:

The closing salutation ends by raising both of your hands (s) above your head. Have the thumbs and fingers touch so that a triangle is formed between them. (t) Smartly drop your hands along the side of your thighs, while simultaneously closing your left foot to your right to form an attention stance. Execute a (u) right front crossover (toward 12 o'clock) with your left open hand over your right clenched fist. Have your (v) left foot step forward (left step through) into a left 45 degree cat stance as you push both of your hands forward (left open hand over right clenched fist) so that they are in line with, and on the same level as, your chin. (w) Step back with your left foot with both your hands opened and placed back-to-back. (x) Slide your right foot back into a right cat stance as you clench both fists in preparation to cocking them to your hips. (y) Shift your right foot alongside of your left foot (attention stance) as you cock both hands (clenched and facing up) to the sides of your waist. (z) Slide your left foot to the left as you drop into a training horse while simultaneously raising both of your hands above your head. Have the thumbs and fingers touch so that a triangle is again formed between them. (aa) Drop both hands to chin level with your left open hand over your right clenched fist. (bb) Have the palms of both of your hands meet (as if praying), and lower them to solar plexus level. (cc) Again raise both of your hands above your head with the thumbs and fingers touching so that they form a triangle between them. (dd) Smartly drop your hands along the side of your thighs, while simultaneously closing your left foot to your right to form an attention stance. (ee) Bow your head. (ff) Lift your head as you end this form in an attention stance.

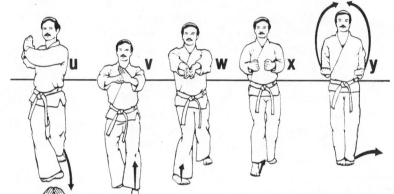

51

# SUMMARY NOTES:

## SHORT FORM 1
1. Practice both sides of the form.
2. Try it in different environments: a smooth floor, on sand, in the dark, in the bathroom, wearing different types of clothing, etc...
3. Practice with attackers with weapons; learn to first block on the outside of their weapons. Repeat the form while blocking on the inside of their weapons.
4. List some of the benefits of covering.
5. Note the advantage of maintaining a consistent head level while moving.
6. Your back elbow strikes should be directed to the rear.
7. Practice the form being conscious of what it is teaching you.
8. List some of the ways the form helps you to improve your freestyle.
9. List some of the ways it improves your fighting.
10. Note the two basic covers in Short Form #1: rear cover and side cover.
11. Practice your blocks utilizing the **DOUBLE FACTOR.**
12. Study the possibilities of executing your inward blocks on the first two moves of the form.

## LONG FORM 1
1. Apply the appropriate ideas from the Notes found in Short Form #1.
2. Practice the form with your eyes closed to gain a better **"FEEL"** for your stances.
3. Perfect the first two inward block-punch sequences because they contain the basic coordination levels of the form.
4. Know when to utilize your hammering inward and your thrusting inward blocks. Be aware of the reason there is a difference.
5. Be sure to keep the heel of your back foot on the ground when you are pivoting into a forward bow. It adds to the push in support of your bracing angle, and stabilizes your stance (base).
6. Economize on the time expended and don't raise the back of your heel when you are executing a step through reverse.
7. What practical application can you affix to the left outward elbow that you used just prior to converting it into your first (left) upward block?
8. When analyzing Long Form #1 please note that the second part of the "Form" is actually the left side of Short Form #1. The only difference is the fact that you are facing 6:00 o'clock while you are utilizing a series of three blocks instead of one.

9. Be sure to have your rear blocking arm cover your entire body when you are employing the series of three blocks during the second part of the form.

10. What reason(s) would you attach to the blocks and punches that stem out of your horse stance at the end of Long Form #1?

11. Be sure to use the *double factor* when blocking. (However when you are executing the *inside downward palm down*, *inside downward palm up*, and *push down blocks*, the *double factor* concept is not in the form).

12. The value of the transition from a neutral bow into a forward bow can be compared to having your foot placed on the wall, then using your foot to help you lunge forward with your punch. As stated above, it adds to the push in support of your bracing angle.

13. Familiarize yourself with *body fusion* and how it can effectively work for you.

14. Practice your punches and gain power through the use of *contouring* both in forward as well as *reverse motion.*

## SHORT FORM 2

1. Be sure to maintain a consistent head level when utilizing your transitional cat stances.

2. The power generated on the third and fourth moves of this Form is similar to the power generated by a tornado. The power is generated from two types of momentum forward and rotational working together to become a destructive force.

3. When you are moving toward 6:00 on the fifth move (and 12:00 o'clock on the sixth move) be sure to emphasize dropping under the punch when you are moving toward the unknown. You should not step into the unknown "*and*" then drop.

4. The middle knuckle strikes on the fifth and sixth moves demonstrate the idea of how to use special weapons for special targets. On your downward "*hairpin*", motion you, are "*nipping the tip*".

5. On the seventh move (and also the eighth) be sure to step forward with your left foot toward 4:30 when you are blocking, and step forward with your right foot toward 4:30, when you are heel palming.

6. Draw half a square on the floor in front of you. Begin by drawing a line from 9 o'clock to 3 o'clock. At the point where you stop, draw a line toward 6 o'clock that is perpendicular to the first line. You now have a geometric model to aid you in checking your stances and your transitions from one stance to another. Begin from your *meditating horse stance* with your right foot in the corner of the half square. When you finish the sixth move of the form your right foot should once again fit in the corner. If not there is an error in your footwork in the first half of the form. Once you are sure the first half of the form is

correct, continue to complete the form. If it is done properly, and *fitted* to your proportions, you should conclude with your right foot in the corner.

7. Derive more meaning from this form by practicing with attackers.

8. It is imperative that you master the opening and closing of your weapons throughout this form. Prevent unnecessary injury to yourself while magnifying the effect of your blocks and strikes.

9. On the ninth and tenth moves of the form, be sure that your inward blocks are executed in a linear manner, and not in a circular manner.

10. Once again, for the best results practice your form in various environments. You will notice a slightly new *feeling*, now that you are moving forward rather than back.

# CHAPTER 4
# PRIORITIES OF SELF-DEFENSE STUDY

As discussed in the study of "Basic Concepts and Principles of Technique", Volume IV, Chapter 7, one basic principle of a technique is often instrumental in triggering another. In studying the functional elements comprising **SELF-DEFENSE TECHNIQUES,** there are sequential priorities that need to be viewed and considered in similar context. Realizing that combat success rests heavily with your ability to maximize all facets of the Art, it stands to reason that you thoroughly study all characteristics that contribute to flexible thought and action. Thus, any condition, function, element, facet, or principle that allows you the ability to instinctively alter, reduce, expand or substitute movements in controlling or increasing your potential effectiveness, needs detailed and serious consideration.

**SELF-DEFENSE** as well as **FREESTYLE TECHNIQUES** share identical functions, elements, facets, and principles. Consequently, as we study both subjects there will be an obvious overlapping of disciplines. Further study will reveal that while selected priorities may vary between the two topics, their disciplines are, nonetheless, consistent in their application. It is also likely that circumstance may cause priorities to vary within each of the topics themselves. The following are priorities that have been selected for **SELF-DEFENSE TECHNIQUES:** (While **FREESTYLE** *priorities* in Chapter 9 are referred to as *considerations,* they are **synonymous** and, therefore, can also apply to **SELF-DEFENSE TECHNIQUES.**)

## ENVIRONMENT

When studying the functional elements comprising **SELF-DEFENSE TECHNIQUES, ENVIRONMENT** should head your list of priorities. This entails total awareness of all *environmental conditions.* It makes into account your overall surroundings -- the floor plan, furniture arrangement, space in which to work; the condition of the terrain (wet, oily, muddy, icy, rough, or smooth); location of objects (walls, stanchions, appliances, tub, toilet, wash basin, street curbs, vehicles); articles (clothes, belt, keys, comb, brush, finger nail file, fork, knife, spoon, pots, pans); your health; your mental condition, etc. -- all of which can work for or against you. More often than not, *environmental conditions* can dictate the strategy, direction, or methods you pursue, or apply in combat. Once you are aware of the benefits of your **ENVIRONMENT,** you soon learn how to use the most inconspicuous articles as weapons, blockades, deterrents, or to learn how to conveniently guide your opponent's targets to chosen obstacles. Even when your health, or mental condition is a factor you learn to overcome and conquer. It is an important aspect of your training worthy of detailed study.

# RANGE

RANGE is second in terms of **SELF-DEFENSE TECHNIQUE** priority. It may already exist when combat commences, thus favoring you, or it may have to be created to insure your safety. Naturally, if **RANGE** is in your favor, you should make every effort to keep it working for you. If it needs to be created, you may do so by moving back, under, above (by jumping, vaulting, or using an overhead beam to pull yourself up) or to either side (right or left) of a strike. Whatever the choice, it is wise to make *distance* become your ally. Try to remember that if an attacker cannot reach you, (providing he has no weapons,) because of the strategic positions created by you, he cannot hurt you. Then too, do not overlook the fact that environmental surroundings, (chairs, tables, posts, etc.,) are excellent blockades to keep an opponent out of reach. Although distances may not be as great, obstacles can be excellent substitutes to keep an opponent from reaching the critical areas of your body.

# POSITION

POSITION is your third order of **SELF-DEFENSE TECHNIQUE** priority. This involves the **POSITION** of your body just before, or during the time of combat. (**POSITIONING** can result from specific **STANCES** that are assumed in combat.) While **POSITION** is influenced by **ENVIRON-MENT** and **RANGE,** it also takes into account the *direction*, as well as the *height, width,* and *depth zones* of your body in relation to your opponent, and his to yours. Should your initial **POSITION** automatically protect you, maintain it. If an attack is eminent, anticipated, or comes as a surprise, instinctively reposition yourself by maneuvering your feet or body to a more protective **POSITION** or to one that allows you instant and effective retaliation. Remember, while proper foot and body maneuvers aid you in repositioning your body to minimize the effects of your opponent's attack, think not only of protection, but also of maintaining easy access to your opponent without loss of continuity and effect.

# FOOT AND HAND POSITIONS

There are only *four basic foot positions* you may place yourself in while fighting. All other foot positions, as you will discover, are no more than variations of the following:

1. **Left to left** - that is your left foot is forward while your opponent's left foot is also in a forward position.

2. **Right to left** - your right foot is forward while your opponent's left foot is still in a forward position.

3. **Left to right** - your left foot is forward while your opponent's right foot is in a forward position.

4. **Right to right** - your right foot is forward while your opponent's right foot is still in a forward position. (See illustrations.)

While the *four basic hand positions*, correspond with the *four basic foot positions* above, hand variations are much more versatile in their use of the dimensions of height, width, and depth. Unlike the feet, which are generally kept on the ground when not kicking, the hands normally follow the pattern of having the lead hand high with the rear hand low *(see illustrations)*. This does

not mean that one couldn't fight from a Cat Stance or a One Leg Stance, and certainly does not preclude the fact that the lead hand could be positioned low and the rear hand high. It must also be pointed out that the position of the feet and hands will alter prior, during, or after their use in offense or defense.

Consider all combinations of **POSITIONS** (this includes postures) you or your opponent may be in during combat (see Volume IV, Chapter 5). Since strikes to various target areas cause reactions that alter **POSITIONS** -- such as bending forward or back, being forced onto the knees, on the hands and knees, stomach, back, etc., -- studying all **POSITIONS** is imperative if you are to instinctively create a tailored response. Making a concentrated effort to learn the various ways in which you can defend yourself, or attack regardless of your or your opponent's **POSITIONS** is the only realistic approach to pursue. While this is only one of the numerous avenues to pursue, it can aid you greatly in creating tactical changes that produce maximum results.

## STANCES

During the course of changing **POSITIONS** and postures (while **MANEUVERING:** by walking, crossing over or back, sliding, shuffling, hopping, skipping, jumping, leaping, or while responding to a strike by bending, falling, etc.,) **STANCES** -- the fourth order of priority -- automatically become by-products of each changing **POSITION.** Isolate each of these **POSITIONS** phonetically and you will unquestionably be able to distinguish between specific **STANCES.** You will discover that within a sequence of **POSITION** changes in motion, transitory **STANCES** invariably occur. While transitory **STANCES** are not intended to be held for any set length of time, they, nevertheless, help the flow and effectiveness of motion. While **MANEUVERING,** a change of hand and body **POSITIONS** should be coordinated with each **STANCE** change. While a particular **STANCE** allows for better protection of the lower regions (target areas) of the body, the fact remains that the hands and body should be **POSITIONED** in preparation for an unanticipated strike, a premeditated attack, or a counterattack. The simultaneous coordination of hand, body, and **STANCE POSITIONS** are of utmost importance and, therefore, cannot be skimmed over. See Volume II, Chapter 6 for more detailed information.

## MANEUVERS

The fifth order of priority is **MANEUVERS.** These are methods that aid you in rapidly changing your **POSITION** to alter, close or extend your **RANGE** (distance). Such knowledge helps to establish fluid movements when you are bobbing, weaving, slipping, advancing, retreating, etc. Mastered, it will minimize your vulnerability, increase your agility, make you elusive, add to your power, accelerate your movements, and frustrate the efforts of your opponent. Refer to Volume II, Chapter 7 for further elaboration.

# TARGETS

POSITIONS and MANEUVERS are prerequisites to a defensive and offensive study of TARGETS -- the sixth priority. POSITIONS and MANEUVERS are useful:

1. Defensive aids that prevent your opponent from striking your TARGETS.
2. Methods that can aid you offensively in striking your opponent's TARGETS.

As indicated, having a thorough knowledge of TARGET AREAS serves a dual purpose. You will know where to strike to obtain maximum results as well as which areas of your body to protect. In retrospect, knowing where to hit can certainly shorten your combat time. Since some TARGET AREAS only require a minimum of force to cause helplessness, it is only logical that you learn where they are located. It would be foolish to repeatedly strike an area that would have little if any effect on your opponent. The study of TARGET AREAS should be viewed from a variety of POSITIONS (this includes postures) you or your opponent may be found in during combat. These POSITIONS may be designed to avoid an attack or cause your opponent to react in a specific way. Whatever your or your opponent's response might be, a change of POSITION automatically alters the location and angle of the TARGET AREA. When this occurs, knowing how to instinctively react to each POSITION change may very likely determine victory.

## ZONE THEORIES

Study of the TARGET AREAS should also include the study of ZONE THEORIES -- the seventh order of priority. Special emphasis should be placed on the DIMENSIONAL ZONE THEORY. This theory is a three dimensional study of an opponent's anatomy and the space surrounding him. It is designed to teach students of *American Kenpo* how to use their imagination to visually divide their opponent's body into vertical and horizontal zones (sections) as viewed from the front, side, or back.

One principle of this theory is to observe ZONES instead of specific TARGET AREAS. Concentrating on one particular TARGET can be risky, especially if your opponent's underlying intent cannot be anticipated. This theory teaches you to encompass the whole and discourages TARGET fixation. However, do not be mislead. Although the TARGET you desire is pinpointed, observing an entire ZONE enables you to totally observe your opponent's intentions.

This theory can also be of benefit in controlling your opponent's natural weapons and **TARGETS** -- while simultaneously preventing your vital **TARGETS** from being hit. Learning to control your opponent's natural weapons, and the **TARGETS** on your body from being struck is a worthwhile endeavor. It is an excellent instructional tool that gives a student a thorough understanding of the countless opportunities that exist in defending or attacking, and how to take advantage of them. Having knowledge of these **ZONES** and the various methods of applying checks and controls makes victory more of a certainty. Refer to Volume IV, Chapters 5 and 6 for a more elaborate explanation of **TARGETS** and **ZONE THEORIES**.

# NATURAL WEAPONS

Obviously the study of the **TARGET AREAS** and **ZONE THEORIES** should also include the study of **NATURAL WEAPONS** -- the eighth order of priority. While knowledge of the vital **TARGET AREAS** tells you where you can hit, knowledge of the **NATURAL WEAPONS**, along with methods and angles of executing them, tells you what **NATURAL WEAPONS** you can expect from your opponent or what you can logically employ to guarantee the best results.

As discussed in Volume 1, Chapter 11, **NATURAL WEAPONS** are those parts of the body that can be transformed into fighting weapons. Knowledge of *what* can be used should also encompass *how* it can be used. Although we may employ the same **NATURAL WEAPONS** to various **TARGETS,** the difference lies in the execution of these **NATURAL WEAPONS**. Techniques utilizing these **NATURAL WEAPONS** vary greatly, so familiarize yourself with them. This added familiarity will magnify your awareness. If your opponent is limited in his knowledge of the uses of his **NATURAL WEAPONS,** your chances of victory are enhanced. Never fail to study, observe, and master other methods of executing the **NATURAL WEAPONS,** nor should you overlook the fact that new methods can be created. You may not believe in a particular method of executing a **NATURAL WEAPON,** but you owe it to yourself to be aware of how it is executed by others so that you'll know how to counter it.

Constantly strive to improve your mastery of the diversified methods of executing **NATURAL WEAPONS.** Every method learned to utilize available **NATURAL WEAPONS** enhances your opportunities to seize the advantage when an opening occurs rather than waiting for another opportunity to present itself. Do not allow this to happen since you may be given only one opportunity.

# NATURAL DEFENSES

**NATURAL DEFENSES** comprise the ninth order of priority. They are the utilization of those parts of your body that can be used to defend yourself. Many of these **NATURAL DEFENSES** are the same parts of the anatomy used as **NATURAL WEAPONS.** However, what determines their use as either a defense or an offense is often the magnitude of force rendered and/or how you check or control your opponent from retaliating. The application of a great deal of force is not necessary when you are executing a block, nor does it require the use of wide or exaggerated movement to be effective. Conserving energy and space in redirecting rather than stopping an attack is generally all that is necessary when you are employing your **NATURAL DEFENSES.** Then too, simple knowledge of how to position your arms or legs rather than synchronizing them with a blow or kick can be an accomplishment in itself.

**NATURAL DEFENSES** are blocks which are primarily defensive moves employing physical contact to check, cushion, deflect, redirect, or stop an offensive move. On other occasions, it can be an anticipated defensive position, which, if correctly planned, can trigger a block. When you are executing a block, physical contact can occur: (1) when force meets force, (2) when force goes with force, (3) when force meets a neutral force, or (4) when a neutral force meets a neutral force. Please refer to Volume III, Chapter 3, for further elaboration.

## BREATHING

**BREATHING** techniques used to insure maximum power in protecting yourself are the tenth order of priority. The importance of proper **BREATHING,** as it relates to the Martial Arts, cannot be overemphasized. To obtain maximum power in all of your endeavors requires proper **BREATHING** habits. A student highly skilled in executing techniques will never perform them with maximum proficiency unless his **BREATHING** is in "sync". Only through timed **BREATHING** can you attain the *spiritual unification* (powers of the mind) and *internal power* known in the Martial Arts as *Chi* or *Ki*.

One area in the Martial Arts where proper **BREATHING** is displayed is in executing the Kiai or Yell. When employing the Kiai, the breath is held and compressed to provide *internal power* for a very short period. Optimum power is available while the breath is retained and by controlling the air that is expelled. Maximum effect stems from unifying all power sources. *Mind, breath* and *strength* must culminate simultaneously. Therefore, when one Kiais in the proper manner, he instantly releases the compressed air within him (measured in terms of a fraction of a second) and simultaneously utilizes his *mental powers* and *physical strength.* Thus, proper synchronization of the above ingredients achieves power beyond the realm of normal execution. Refer to Volume IV, Chapter 3, for a more detailed account on **BREATHING.**

# TAILORING

**TAILORING** the art is the eleventh priority. Because each of us is physiologically and anatomically different, all basic moves should be **TAILORED** to suit us individually. While many traditionalists challenge this theory, students, nevertheless, achieve proficiency beyond their expected levels. It is extremely misleading to force a student to execute a move in only one way. He can be taught a specific, exclusive way at first only if it is used as a *point of reference.* Once referenced, moves should then be modified to harmonize with the physical make-up of each student. As each learning process is adjusted to the individual, students should then be informed that while identical ingredients to successful learning may apply to all, the proportion will vary according to a student's natural inherent qualities. Similar or identical principles may be learned, but when applied, the formula will vary with each individual.

As a student learns a system, he gradually develops his own style. In defining the words system and style, it can be said that a system is the unification of related ideas, concepts, theories, principles, facts, truths, and the basic elements of a particular school of Martial Arts. These methods are usually arranged in a progressive and logical manner to make learning easy. The basic criteria of a good system rests with the number of variables that it offers. If its methods are inclusive and practical, you can expect positive results in combat.

Style is a word used to describe the manner in which an individual applies and executes the system he has learned. It is no more than one's method of executing a particular move, maneuver, assignment, chore, etc. It is the method used by the individual while hammering a nail if he is a carpenter, using a brush to paint with if he is an artist, or applying strikes if he is a Martial Artist. While we are writing, it is our method of executing the pen or pencil that makes our penmanship distinctive and unique in style. As an example, although our signature varies a little each time we write it, nevertheless, it is unquestionably identifiable as our style of writing. Refer to Volume I, Chapter 8 for a more detailed explanation.

As a student slowly digests the system he is studying, he will invariably convert the movements he has learned into a style which is characteristic of him. This evolution must take place if the student desires to achieve his full potential. When this occurs, the execution of his movements will appear different from the rest of his colleagues. However, while the outward appearance of a move may seem different when you are comparing one student with another, the underlying principle within the move repeatedly remains unchanged. Therefore, if a move changes in appearance, yet gives maximum effectiveness without changing the underlying principle, it is correct. In short, "Like a custom tailor who fits a suit to an individual, so should an instructor fit the Art to an individual."

**TAILORING** encompasses a number of basic concepts. Two of these concepts place emphasis not only on how your moves are to be **TAILORED** to you, but how they can be **TAILORED** to your opponent. These two concepts teach you to use the *contour* of both your body and your opponent's body to enhance your action. Using the *contour* of your body to guide, launch, conserve, and control your natural weapons, teaches you that when you confine your moves to your own gravitational field, you proportionately maximize your force. Once this is learned, knowledge of how to use the *contour* of your opponent's body to your advantage is the next logical stage of progression. **CONTOUR** refers to the outline of an opponent's body, or yours, no matter what **POSITION** or posture you may find him or yourself in.

The concepts of **TAILORING** go beyond simple application. Amply stated by Tom Riskas in his Thesis for Fourth Degree Black Belt, "One's formal training, then, is a function of physical conditioning and the effective *tailoring* of various ideas and concepts to the individual's mental and physical capacity." He further stated that the key words to the above statement are: "Idea, *tailoring* and capacity." In order to develop individuality to its utmost, he stressed the point that. . "the instructor should strive to adapt (*tailor*) the basic idea or concept to the student's capacity, i.e., his individuality. Failure to do so grossly violates the essence of defense technique training."

**SELF-DEFENSE TECHNIQUE** training gives definition and meaning to basic fundamentals. Although each technique sequence is different, it follows a logical and systematic pattern that can provide basic fundamentals in combat. Realizing that no two situations are alike in combat, the predetermined moves contained within a technique are taught to be viewed as a *conceptual idea* that can be *tailored* to suit each changing situation. One learns that *it is the conceptual framework of the technique that constitutes the idea.* The technique is not meant to be executed in perfect sequence, but rather represents an *idea* which can develop individuality. As a student develops latitude and flexibility through practice, he can instinctively draw upon his *ideas* and *tailor* them to suit his needs. Individuality gives latitude and flexibility which in turn allows him to rearrange, modify, expand, condense or delete basics and still preserve maximum effectiveness. Students who are, therefore, armed with a comprehensive vocabulary of movement can extemporaneously utilize their basics and be effective regardless of the situation.

**SELF-DEFENSE TECHNIQUE** study, however, requires dedication as well as analyzation -- not memorization. While it is a natural tendency for beginners to want to memorize technique sequences, they should be taught to view the sequences and particulars of a technique as incidental to the basic ideas and concepts involved. They should be more concerned with the consistent logic contained within the basic concepts involved and not subjected to an unyielding commitment. Unyielding commitments only restrict *instinctive tailoring.*

Detailed study of practical concepts and principles of attack and defense as well as the variables associated with each type of attack or defense is the real key. As you further examine the functions of each of the variables, you learn the true meaning of latitude and flexibility, all of which complement the concepts of **TAILORING.** This is especially true when your very existence requires an instinctively correct reaction.

Preservation, therefore, rests with a favorable alternate response. Alternate changes must be done instinctively and spontaneously to be conclusively effective. That is the reason why memorization is not enough. Sequential alternatives should be viewed and studied from as many practical combinations as possible. More often than not, moves learned in one technique will blend with those of another so that in time, alternate techniques are no more than components of the techniques learned.

As a result of adding the practical viewpoint to the classical methods of old, defense techniques have thus taken on a new and realistic dimension in today's society. Strict alliance to traditional (classical) methods not only restricts creativity and self expression, but often fails to blend with our ever changing environment. Confine your horizons of latitude and flexibility and you automatically restrict your ability to randomly *tailor* the Art in achieving victory. Allow for latitude and flexibility and you will reap the benefits of instinctive **TAILORING.**

# PHYSICAL AND MENTAL CONDITIONING

Both **PHYSICAL AND MENTAL CONDITIONING** make up the twelfth priority. Obviously, the training with, and the study of **STANCES, MANEUVERS, NATURAL WEAPONS** and **DEFENSES** automatically **CONDITION** you **PHYSICALLY** and **MENTALLY.** As you delve into the intricacies of body movements and the functions of the mind, sophistication inevitably emerges at each stage of progression. The more time and effort you devote, the greater the sophistication. Such development can only come through dedicated training and detailed analyzation of all practical aspects of the Art.

Like all physical activity, training is a prerequisite for proficiency. This entails the **CONDITIONING** of the muscles, joints, and other parts of the body so that they function with proficiency in the midst of an attack. However, **MENTAL CONDITIONING** is also essential if you expect to totally maximize your physical efforts. Marriage of the mind and body is imperative. Harmoniously working with your **BREATH,** they develop your skills to a point of superior physical sensitivity and mental instinctiveness. While the body reaches heights of conditioned response, the mind ultimately transcends to a state of superconsciousness. At this stage, strategies and plans of defense and offense are not thought of consciously -- they happen naturally.

Properly trained, **MENTALLY** as well as **PHYSICALLY,** your body and mind will automatically respond to any given situation. Arrive at this level and you will witness a period in your development where many of your senses will peak beyond your expectations. You'll be able to sense, feel, and smell trouble, and magnify your sense of touch, sight and hearing. Refer to Volume IV, Chapters 2 and 4 for a more detailed explanation.

# CHAPTER 5
# NATURE OF THE ATTACK

In studying the **NATURE OF THE ATTACK,** you must learn to: (1) identify, define and classify the types of encounters you may find yourself in; (2) thoroughly scrutinize the various methods in which weapons (natural or otherwise) can be employed; and (3) instinctively determine your choice of action in successfully combating the numerous types of encounters with which you may be confronted.

When identifying the **NATURE OF THE ATTACK,** you must first ascertain whether trouble is (1) eminent in the **ENVIRONMENT** you are entering; then (2) anticipate the possibility of an encounter; and (3) eliminate the element of surprise. Although the type of action you encounter may surprise you, you would, nevertheless, be prepared to instinctively utilize your knowledge regardless of the predicament. Again, at this stage, strategy and plans for defense and offense are not thought of consciously -- they occur naturally.

Defining the predicament involves classifying and categorizing the various types of attack. Answers are more appropriately geared to attack situations when they are categorized into topics such as:

1. *Grabs and Tackles*
2. *Pushes*
3. *Punches*
4. *Kicks*
5. *Holds and Hugs*
6. *Locks and Chokes*
7. *Weapons*
8. *Multiple Attacks*

While these categories become extremely helpful in defining the attack, they, nevertheless, are general categories. Specific detailing is needed since there are numerous methods of executing the techniques listed in each category. Examples of specific detailing will be discussed later in the chapter.

In my determination to classify and categorize the various types of attacks in a logical and systematic order I was prompted to create the **WEB OF KNOWLEDGE.**

# WEB OF KNOWLEDGE

The idea for the **WEB OF KNOWLEDGE** came to me twenty six years ago in Hawaii as I observed a spider constructing a web. As I watched the spider meticulously build this ingenious trap for his survival, I attempted to parallel the principles of this construction with the learning of the Martial Arts. From this design created by our Supreme Being, I pondered about how it could be used as a beneficial trap: a trap that would be an aid in retaining Martial Arts' knowledge. Surely, if a web is primarily a trap to ensnare victims, why couldn't a similar structure be used to ensnare knowledge? As I began to develop the concept, I pondered about topics that could be studied. What knowledge was the web to contain and what order of priority would it follow? Would the topics of study vary from one belt level to another? If so, what belonged where? Such unanswered questions did not make it easy to create and organize a progressive plan utilizing a **WEB OF KNOWLEDGE.** Through trial and error, I arrived at what I thought to be an effective solution. I categorized the web into prime topics of concern and arranged the course in a manner that I considered progressive.

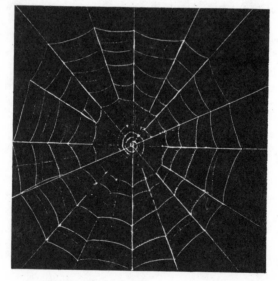

The *Web* is prioritized according to the degree of difficulty in handling an attack:

1. **Grabs and Tackles** -- The beginning student should have a good chance against a grab where the opponent does not instantly plan a punch. Without an immediate follow-up, a grab is basically inactive.

**2. Pushes** -- Because of the forward momentum of pushes, their counters require better timing than those for grabs, but not as much as the required timing for a punch.

**3. Punches** -- Still a greater degree of timing is required to block this attack due to the faster speed and force of a punch.

**4. Kicks** -- Not only do kicks require timing, but they have potentially greater power than punches -- thus making them more dangerous.

**5. Holds and Hugs** -- These in turn are more difficult because of the restriction of body movement and the limited number of available weapons and targets, as well as a real danger of being taken to the ground.

**6. Chokes and Locks** -- These are more dangerous than Holds and Hugs as they have the potential for causing broken limbs and even instant death.

**7. Weapons** -- The timing and power associated with weapons easily rates them as being the most difficult to handle. Your opponent has a range advantage with a high probability of serious injury or death.

**8. Multiple Attacks** -- Defense against multiple attacks require skill and strategy. Being attacked by more than one opponent increases the probability of serious injury or death and, therefore, should be viewed as being equivalent to a single attacker well versed in the use of a weapon.

**9. Combinations of the Above** -- Other combinations should also be considered, such as a *grab with a punch, a choke with a knife pressed against you, being grabbed by one opponent and attacked by another with a weapon*, etc.

Careful examination of the techniques required in each of the belt levels will reveal that the topics listed above are in the exact order in which I introduce techniques to my students. While all belt levels up through Green Belt, in my schools as well as other IKKA affiliates, follow the same sequence of topics, there are noticeable omissions of attacks within the sequence of some of the belt levels. The omission of various attacks within the sequence may be due to the frequency of different attacks. Lower belt requirements may stress more grabs, punches, hugs, or holds since there is a greater probability of encountering these types of attacks rather than kicks. Secondly, beginners are not totally equipped to make kicking and weapon techniques work because of their limited experience.

# HOW TO READ THE WEB OF KNOWLEDGE

The following illustration should be an aid in understanding the basic **structure of the WEB.** When I designed the **WEB,** I placed the topics of concern, in the spaces *indicated by the arrows*. These topics were arranged categorically according to the degree of difficulty required in handling an attack. To enhance student learning, I placed specific techniques (*indicated by the numbers*) under each of the topics. I then selected the most elementary technique from each of the topics (proceeded in a clockwise manner) and arranged them accordingly. This not only allowed the student to learn a technique from each of the categories, but as the procedure of selection continued, more sophisticated techniques were introduced.

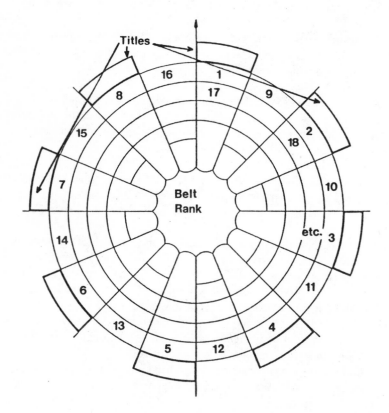

# REQUIRED TECHNIQUES FOR YELLOW BELT
(In the order they are to be taught)

1. **DELAYED SWORD** (front - right hand lapel grab)
2. **ALTERNATING MACES** (front - two-hand push)
3. **SWORD OF DESTRUCTION** (front - left straight or roundhouse punch)
4. **DEFLECTING HAMMER** (front - right front thrust kick)
5. **CAPTURED TWIGS** (rear - bear-hug, arms pinned)
6. **THE GRASP OF DEATH** (left flank - right arm headlock)
7. **CHECKING THE STORM** (front - right step-through overhead club)
8. **MACE OF AGGRESSION** (front - two-hand lapel grab, pulling in)
9. **ATTACKING MACE** (front - right step-through straight punch)
10. **SWORD AND HAMMER** (right flank - left hand shoulder grab)

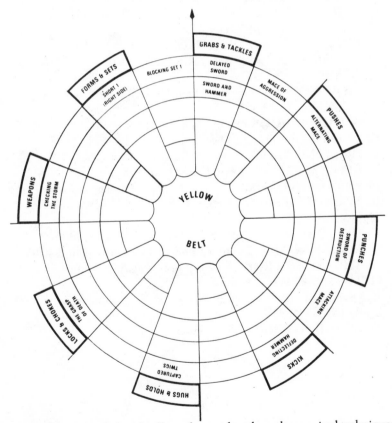

Follow the yellow belt web of knowlege and see how the required techniques were numbered.

# REQUIRED TECHNIQUES FOR ORANGE BELT
(In the order they are to be taught)

1. **CLUTCHING FEATHERS** - Front Left Hand Hair Grab
2. **TRIGGERED SALUTE** - Front Right Hand Direct Push
3. **DANCE OF DEATH** - Front Right Straight Punch
4. **THRUSTING SALUTE** - Front Right Step Through Kick
5. **GIFT OF DESTRUCTION** - Handshake
6. **LOCKING HORNS** - Front Headlock
7. **LONE KIMONO** - Front Left Hand Lapel Grab
8. **GLANCING SALUTE** - Front Right Hand Cross Push
9. **FIVE SWORDS** - Front Right Step Through Roundhouse Punch
10. **BUCKLING BRANCH** - Front Left Step Through Kick
11. **SCRAPING HOOF** - Full Nelson
12. **GRIP OF DEATH** - Left Flank Right Arm Headlock
13. **CROSSING TALON** - Front Right Cross Wrist Grab
14. **REPEATING MACE** - Front Left Hand Push
15. **SHIELDING HAMMER** - Front Left Step Through Hooking Punch
16. **STRIKING SERPENT'S HEAD** - Front Bear Hug, Arms Free
17. **LOCKED WING** - Hammerlock
18. **OBSCURE WING** - Right Flank Left Hand Shoulder Grab
19. **REVERSING MACE** - Front Left Step Through Straight Punch
20. **THRUSTING PRONGS** - Front Bear Hug, Arms Pinned
21. **TWISTED TWIG** - Front Wrist Lock
22. **OBSCURE SWORD** - Right Flank Left Hand Shoulder Grab
23. **RAINING CLAW** - Front Right Uppercut Punch
24. **CRASHING WINGS** - Rear Bear Hug, Arms Free

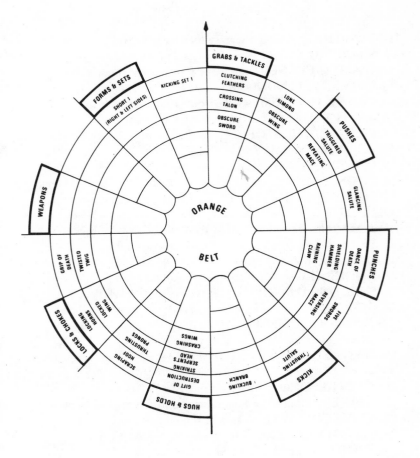

GRABS & TACKLES

CLUTCHING FEATHERS
CROSSING TALON
OBSCURE SWORD

LONE KIMONO
OBSCURE WING

PUSHES

TRIGGERED SALUTE
REPEATING MACE
GLANCING SALUTE

FORMS & SETS

KICKING SET 1
SHORT 1 (RIGHT & LEFT SIDES)

ORANGE

BELT

PUNCHES

SHIELDING HAMMER
DANCE OF DEATH
RAINING CLAW
REVERSING MACE
FIVE SWORDS

WEAPONS

GRIP OF DEATH
TWISTED TWIG

LOCKS & CHOKES

LOCKING WING
LOCKED WING

HUGS & HOLDS

SCRAPING HOOF
THRUSTING PRONGS
CRASHING WINGS
STRIKING SERPENT'S HEAD
GIFT OF DESTRUCTION

KICKS

THRUSTING SALUTE
BUCKING BRANCH

## REQUIRED TECHNIQUES FOR PURPLE BELT
(In the order they are to be taught)

1. **TWIRLING WINGS** - Rear Two-Hand Stiff-Arm Shoulder Grab
2. **SNAPPING TWIG** - Front Left Hand Chest Push
3. **LEAPING CRANE** - Front Right Step Through Punch
4. **SWINGING PENDULUM** - Front Right Roundhouse Kick
5. **CRUSHING HAMMER** - Rear Bear Hug--Arms Pinned
6. **CAPTURED LEAVES** - Right Flank Finger Lock
7. **EVADING THE STORM** - Front Right Step Through Overhead Club
8. **CHARGING RAM** - Front Tackle
9. **PARTING WINGS** - Front Two-Hand Push
10. **THUNDERING HAMMERS** - Front Right Step Through Punch
11. **SQUEEZING THE PEACH** - Rear Bear Hug--Arms Pinned
12. **CIRCLING WING** - Rear Two-Hand Choke--Arms Bent
13. **CALMING THE STORM** - Front Right Step Through Roundhouse Club
14. **DARTING MACE** - Front Two-Hand Wrist Grab
15. **HOOKING WINGS** - Front Two-Hand Low Push
16. **SHIELD AND SWORD** - Front Left Step Through Punch
17. **GIFT IN RETURN** - Front Handshake
18. **BOW OF COMPULSION** - Front Wrist Lock Against Opponent's Chest
19. **OBSTRUCTING THE STORM** - Front Right Step Through Overhead Club
20. **TWIN KIMONO** - Front Two-Hand Lapel Grab--Push Out
21. **SLEEPER** - Front Right Front Step Through Straight Punch
22. **SPIRALING TWIG** - Rear Bear Hug--Arms Free
23. **CROSS OF DESTRUCTION** - Rear Two-Hand Choke
24. **FLIGHT TO FREEDOM** - Rear Hammerlock

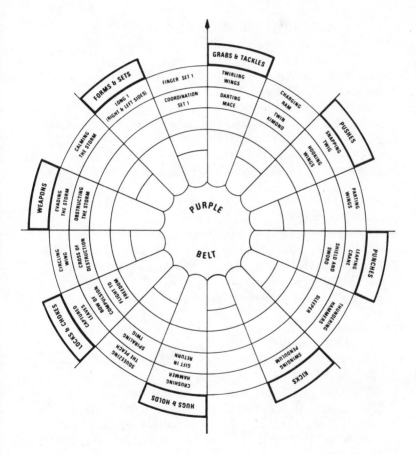

## REQUIRED TECHNIQUES FOR BLUE BELT
(In the order they are to be taught)

1. **BEGGING HANDS** - Front Two-Hand Grab to Wrists
2. **THRUSTING WEDGE** - Front Two-Hand High Push
3. **FLASHING WINGS** - Front Right Step Through Punch
4. **HUGGING PENDULUM** - Front Right Thrusting Knife-Edge Kick
5. **REPEATED DEVASTATION** - Full Nelson
6. **ENTANGLED WING** - Front Arm Lock
7. **DEFYING THE STORM** - Front Right Step Through Roundhouse Club
8. **RAKING MACE** - Front Two-Hand Lapel Grab -- Pulling In
9. **SNAKING TALON** - Front Two-Hand Push
10. **SHIELD AND MACE** - Front Right Step Through Punch
11. **RETREATING PENDULUM** - Front Right Thrusting Heel Kick
12. **TRIPPING ARROW** - Front Bear Hug Arms Free
13. **FALLEN CROSS** - Rear Two-Hand Choke
14. **RETURNING STORM** - Front Inward Roundhouse And Backhand Club
15. **CROSSED TWIGS** - Rear Two-Hand Grab to Wrists
16. **TWIST OF FATE** - Front Two-Hand Push
17. **FLASHING MACE** - Front Right Step Through Punch
18. **GIFT OF DESTINY** - Front Handshake
19. **WINGS OF SILK** - Rear Two-Arm Armlock
20. **GRIPPING TALON** - Front Left Direct Right Wrist Grab
21. **GATHERING CLOUDS** - Front Right Step Through Punch
22. **DESTRUCTIVE TWINS** - Front Two-Hand Choke -- Pulling In
23. **BROKEN RAM** - Front Tackle
24. **CIRCLING THE HORIZON** - Front Right Step Through Punch

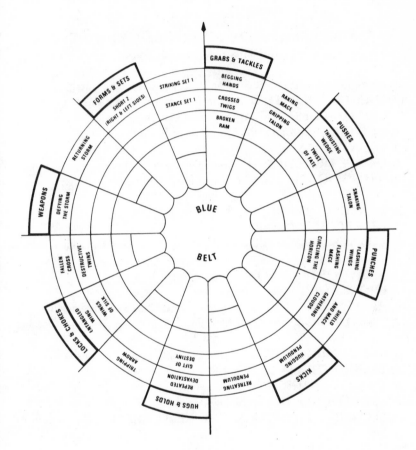

GRABS & TACKLES

FORMS & SETS

PUSHES

WEAPONS

PUNCHES

LOCKS & CHOKES

KICKS

HUGS & HOLDS

BLUE BELT

STRIKING SET 1

STANCE SET 1

BEGGING HANDS

CROSSED TWIGS

BROKEN RAM

RAKING MACE

GRIPPING TALON

TWIST OF FATE

THRUSTING WEDGE

SNAKING TALON

FLASHING WINGS

CIRCLING THE HORIZON

FLASHING MACE

GATHERING CLOUDS

SHIELD AND MACE

HUGGING PENDULUM

RETREATING PENDULUM

REPEATED DEVASTATION

GIFT OF DESTINY

TRIPPING ARROW

ENTANGLED WING

WING OF SILK

DESTRUCTIVE TWINS

FALLEN CROSS

DEFYING THE STORM

RETURNING STORM

SHORT 2 (RIGHT & LEFT SIDES)

## REQUIRED TECHNIQUES FOR GREEN BELT
(In the order they are to be taught)

1. **OBSCURE CLAWS** - Right Flank Left Hand Shoulder Grab
2. **ENCOUNTER WITH DANGER** - Front Two-Hand Push
3. **CIRCLING DESTRUCTION** - Front Left Step Through Punch
4. **DETOUR FROM DOOM** - Front Right Roundhouse Kick
5. **SQUATTING SACRIFICE** - Rear Bear Hug-- Arms Free
6. **ESCAPE FROM DEATH** - Rear Right-Arm Choke
7. **BRUSHING THE STORM** - Right Flank Right Step Through Overhead Club
8. **MENACING TWIRL** - Rear Left Hand Belt Grab
9. **LEAP FROM DANGER** - Rear Two-Hand Push
10. **CIRCLES OF PROTECTION** - Front Right Step Through Overhead Punch
11. **CIRCLE OF DOOM** - Front Right Straight Kick
12. **BROKEN GIFT** - Front Handshake
13. **HEAVENLY ASCENT** - Front Two-Hand Choke--Arms Straight
14. **CAPTURING THE STORM** - Front Right Step Through Overhead Club
15. **CONQUERING SHIELD** - Front Left Stiff-Arm Lapel Grab
16. **TAMING THE MACE** - Front Right Step Through Punch
17. **TWIRLING SACRIFICE** - Full Nelson
18. **CROSS OF DEATH** - Front Two-Hand Cross Choke
19. **SECURING THE STORM** - Front Right Step Through Roundhouse Club
20. **INTERCEPTING THE RAM** - Front Tackle
21. **KNEEL OF COMPULSION** - Right Flank Right Step Through Punch
22. **CLIPPING THE STORM** - Front Right Thrusting Club
23. **GLANCING WING** - Front Left Uppercut Punch
24. **THE BACK BREAKER** - Right Flank Right Step Through Punch

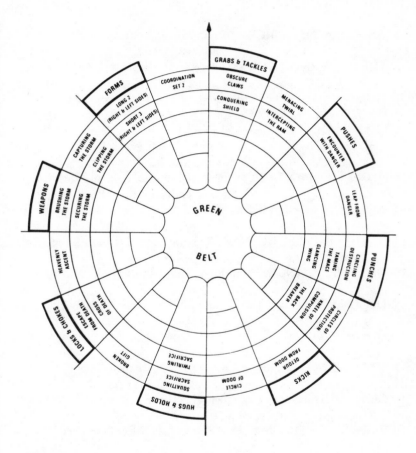

FORMS

GRABS & TACKLES

PUSHES

PUNCHES

KICKS

HUGS & HOLDS

LOCKS & CHOKES

WEAPONS

GREEN

BELT

COORDINATION SET 2

OBSCURE CLAWS

MENACING TWIRL

CONQUERING SHIELD

INTERCEPTING THE RAM

ENCOUNTER WITH DANGER

LEAP FROM DANGER

CIRCLING DESTRUCTION

TAMING THE MACE

GLANCING WING

THE BACK BREAKER

TWIN KICKS OF COMPULSION

PROTECTION OF DETOUR FROM DOOM

CIRCLE OF DOOM

TWIRLING SACRIFICE

SQUATTING SACRIFICE

BROKEN GIFT

GIFT OF DEATH

ESCAPE FROM DEATH

HEAVENLY ASCENT

BRUSHING THE STORM

SECURING THE STORM

CAPTURING THE STORM

CLIPPING THE STORM

LONG 2 (RIGHT & LEFT SIDES)

SHORT 3 (RIGHT & LEFT SIDES)

# REQUIRED TECHNIQUES FOR 3RD DEGREE BROWN BELT
(In the order they are to be taught)

1. **GLANCING SPEAR** - Front Right Direct Left Wrist Grab
2. **THRUST INTO DARKNESS** - Rear Right Step Through Punch
3. **CIRCLING FANS** - Front Right And Left Front Straight Punch Combination
4. **ROTATING DESTRUCTION** - Front Right Snap and Left Spinning Back Kicks
5. **FALCONS OF FORCE** - Flank Left and Right Shoulder Grab By Two Men
6. **THE BEAR AND THE RAM** - Front Right Punch and Rear Bear Hug -- Arms Free
7. **RAINING LANCE** - Front Right Step Through Overhead Knife
8. **DESPERATE FALCONS** - Front Two-Hand Grab To Both Wrists
9. **LEAP OF DEATH** - Front Right Step Through Punch
10. **PROTECTING FANS** - Front Right & Left Punch Combination With Opponent's Left Leg Forward
11. **DECEPTIVE PANTHER** - Combination Right Front Snap Kick (Low) & Right Roundhouse Kick (High)
12. **COURTING THE TIGER** - Flank Left & Right Arm Grabs By Two Men
13. **GATHERING OF THE SNAKES** - Front Left Punch & Rear Right Punch By Two Men
14. **GLANCING LANCE** - Front Right Knife Thrust While Your Arms Are Down
15. **DOMINATING CIRCLES** - Front Right Shoulder Grab By Opponent's Right Hand
16. **DESTRUCTIVE FANS** - Left Flank Right Punch With Opponent's Right Leg Forward
17. **UNFURLING CRANE** - Front Right & Left Punch Combination With Opponent's Right Leg Forward
18. **GRASPING EAGLES** - Front Right Lapel Grab & Rear Right Arm Grab By Two Men
19. **PARTING OF THE SNAKES** - Front Right Punch & Rear Attempt By Two Men
20. **THRUSTING LANCE** - Front Right Knife Thrust While Your Arms Are Down
21. **BLINDING SACRIFICE** - Front Two-Hand Grab Or Choke
22. **SNAKES OF WISDOM** - Flank Left & Right Shoulder Grabs By Two Men
23. **ENTWINED LANCE** - Front Right Knife Thrust
24. **FALLING FALCON** - Front Right Direct Lapel Grab

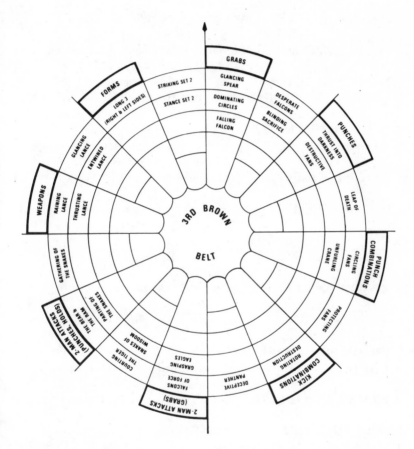

**GRABS**
- GLANCING SPEAR
- DOMINATING CIRCLES
- FALLING FALCON
- DESPERATE FALCONS
- BLINDING SACRIFICE

**FORMS**
- STRIKING SET 2
- STANCE SET 2
- LONG 3 (RIGHT & LEFT SIDES)

**WEAPONS**
- GLANCING LANCE
- ENTWINED LANCE
- RAINING LANCE
- THRUSTING LANCE

**PUNCHES**
- THRUST INTO DARKNESS
- DESTRUCTIVE FANS
- LEAP OF DEATH

**PUNCH COMBINATIONS**
- CIRCLING FANS
- UNFURLING CRANE

**3RD BROWN BELT**

**2-MAN ATTACKS (PUNCHES, HOLDS)**
- GATHERING OF THE SNAKES
- THE BEAR & PARTING OF THE SNAKES

**2-MAN ATTACKS (GRABS)**
- COURTING THE TIGER
- SNAKES OF WISDOM
- GRASPING EAGLES
- FALCONS OF FORCE
- DECEPTIVE PANTHER

**KICK COMBINATIONS**
- PROTECTING FANS
- ROTATING DESTRUCTION

81

## REQUIRED TECHNIQUES FOR 2ND DEGREE BROWN BELT
(In the order they are to be taught)

1. **FATAL CROSS** - Front Two-Hand Attempted Low Grab Or Push
2. **TWIRLING HAMMERS** - Front Left Step Through Punch
3. **DEFENSIVE CROSS** - Front Right Snap Kick
4. **DANCE OF DARKNESS** - Front Right Kick Followed By A Right Punch
5. **MARRIAGE OF THE RAMS** - Right & Left Shoulder Grabs (Close) By Two Men
6. **THE RAM AND THE EAGLE** - Front Right Punch & Rear Left Collar Grab By Two Men
7. **ESCAPE FROM THE STORM** - Right Flank Right Overhead Club
8. **CIRCLING WINDMILLS** - Front Two-Hand Push Followed By A Right Punch
9. **DESTRUCTIVE KNEEL** - Front Right Step Through Punch
10. **BOWING TO BUDDHA** - Front Right Roundhouse Kick (While Kneeling On Ground)
11. **REVERSING CIRCLES** - Front Left Roundhouse Kick Followed By A Left Punch
12. **REPRIMANDING THE BEARS** - Front Right Punch & Rear Bear Hug By Two Men -- Arms, Free
13. **CIRCLING THE STORM** - Front Right Club Thrust (Poke)
14. **UNFOLDING THE DARK** - Left Step Through Punch From The Right Rear Flank
15. **UNWINDING PENDULUM** - Front Right Kick Followed By A Right Punch
16. **PIERCING LANCE** - Front Right Knife Thrust While Your Arms Are Up
17. **ESCAPE FROM DARKNESS** - Right Punch From Left Rear Flank
8. **CAPTURING THE ROD** - Front Right Pistol Holdup (Against Your Chest)
9. **PRANCE OF THE TIGER** - Right Flank Right Step Through Uppercut Punch
20. **BROKEN ROD** - Rear Right Hand Pistol
21. **ENTWINED MACES** - Front Right & Left Front Punch With Opponent's Left Leg Forward
22. **DEFYING THE ROD** - Front Right Pistol Holdup
23. **FATAL DEVIATION** - Front Right & Left Punch With Opponent's Left Leg Forward
24. **TWISTED ROD** - Front Right Pistol Holdup

PUSHES
FORMS
PUNCHES
WEAPONS
KICKS
COMBINATIONS PUNCHES/HOLDS 2-MAN
2-MAN (GRABS)
KICK PUNCH COMBINATIONS

TWO MAN SET (BOTH SIDES)
FATAL CROSS
CIRCLING WINDMILLS
FORM 4
CIRCLING THE STORM
TWIRLING HAMMERS
UNFOLDING THE DARK
PRANCE OF THE TIGER
CAPTURING THE ROD
DEFYING THE ROD
DESTRUCTIVE KNEEL
ESCAPE FROM DARKNESS
ESCAPE FROM THE STORM
PIERCING LANCE
BROKEN ROD
TWISTED ROD

2ND BROWN
BELT

DEFENSIVE CROSS
REPRIMANDING THE BEARS
THE EAGLE
BOWING TO BUDDA
THE RAM
FATAL DEVIATION
ENTWINED MACES
UNWINDING PENDULUM
DANCE OF DARKNESS
MARRIAGE OF THE RAMS
REVERSING CIRCLES

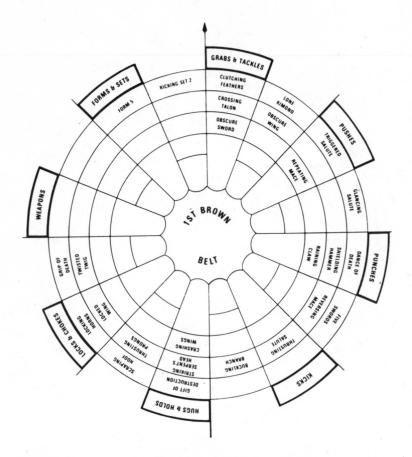

**NOTE:** The *techniques* for **FIRST DEGREE BROWN** are identical to those listed under the **ORANGE BELT** requirements. The only difference is that the *techniques* in **FIRST DEGREE BROWN** extend beyond **ORANGE** for purposes of introducing newer concepts and principles of motion.

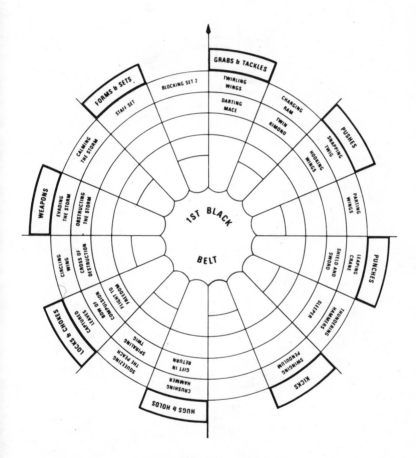

**NOTE:** The *techniques* for **FIRST DEGREE BLACK** are identical to those listed under the **PURPLE BELT** requirements. **FIRST DEGREE BLACK** requirements are extensions of the **PURPLE BELT**. They also introduce newer concepts and principles of motion.

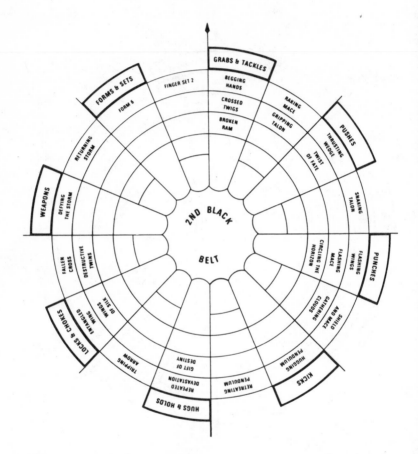

**NOTE:** The *techniques* for **SECOND DEGREE BLACK** are identical to those listed under the **BLUE BELT** requirements. **SECOND DEGREE BLACK** requirements are extensions of your **BLUE BELT.** Study the concepts and principles that are offered.

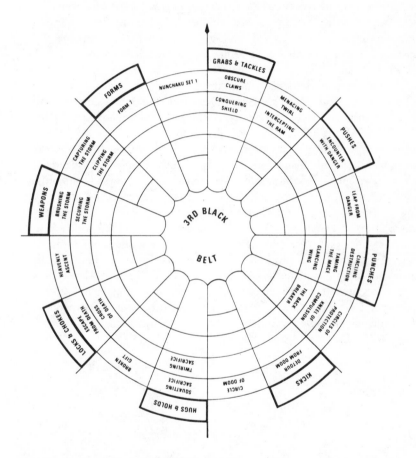

**NOTE:** The *techniques* for **THIRD DEGREE BLACK** are identical to those listed under the **GREEN BELT** requirements. It, too, extends beyond the **GREEN** for purposes of introducing newer concepts and principles of motion.

Besides understanding the relative difficulty and danger of various attacks, you should explore related usages for the *Web* by visualizing and categorizing the various attacks according to direction, method, path, dimension, and angle of delivery or execution. For example, a punch might be delivered with a left or right hand, in a linear or circular motion while employing a variety of methods. Such methods of execution may: (1) create straight, hook, or roundhouse punches; (2) employ related methods in the form of a cross, jab, uppercut, chop, rake, or thrust type punches; or they may require (3) delivering punches with the rear or lead hand while in a stationary position, shuffling, or using a step through maneuver; or (4) by using combinations of the same. All methods of punching, grabbing, pushing, etc., and their combinations should be studied.

The greater your knowledge of existing methods, the greater your repertoire of knowledge -- all of which lessens your chances of being surprised. All motions that have been discussed may be compatibly inserted into the **UNIVERSAL PATTERN** (Volume IV, Chapter 8).

In time you will learn that a specific technique used for a right hand grab may be suitably or identically used for a right hand push or punch. It may require altering the timing of your action, but you, nevertheless, would still employ the identical technique pattern. When the structure of a technique allows for identical use against each of the types of linear motion mentioned, spontaneity is proportionately increased. There is no hesitation in deciding which technique to use, you simply respond to the action without deviating from the prescribed pattern. The substitution of a knife, however, would undoubtedly alter your technique pattern.

Sophisticated strategy would be needed to control your opponent's actions. Naturally, logic should always dictate your need to alter, reduce, expand, or substitute your movements to increase your chances of success.

# CHAPTER 6
# AN ANALYTICAL STUDY OF MOTION

When you are studying the various ways in which weapons (natural or otherwise) can be employed, you should analyze the intricacies of motion itself. You should familiarize yourself with all aspects contained in motion as well as affected by motion. Like all studies, a sequential order of priority invariably affords a more favorable approach when you are trying to fully grasp a specific subject. Therefore, I will now attempt to sequentially discuss the composition of motion. To best understand motion, analysis should encompass:

1. **Direction**
2. **Method**
3. **Path**
4. **Dimension**
5. **Angle**

*Direction* involves the direction from which you or your opponent's action may stem. Such action may be restricted or complemented by the location of the person(s) involved, or because of the location of environmental objects. If the location of the person(s) or objects restricts your action, you would then be limited and compelled to seek other courses of action. Action, therefore, can stem from several directions:

1. **Front**
2. **Back**
3. **Left Side**
4. **Right Side**
5. **Above (up)**
6. **Below (down)**

Although the above terms are simply stated as front, back, left side, right side, above (up) or below (down), further elaboration is needed to fully understand the actual involvement of these simple terms.

Front and back encompasses both direction and location. What differntiates between direction and location is your selection of who or what is considered to be your point of reference. For example, if you were to start with yourself as the point of reference when you are confronted by an opponent, then the terms front or back would refer to the location of your opponent in relation to you. Direction, however, specifically pinpoints where your opponent is located when he is in front of you, to your back, or to your side. Location is general, direction is more specific. Using the *"clock principle"* (see Volume II, Chapter 4) you would know specifically where your opponent was located in relation to the clock, such as 12, 3, 6, 9 o'clock, etc. To refresh your memory, the "clock principle" suggests that a student picture himself standing in the middle of a large clock that has been placed on the floor (*see illustration*)

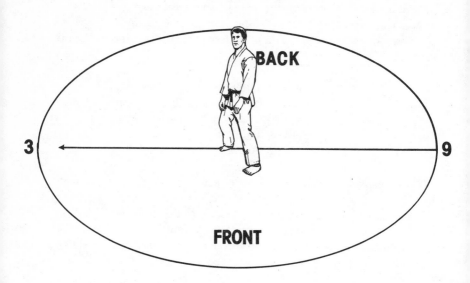

or is standing upright if this is preferable. Using this mental aid enables a student to properly position his feet or hands in performing his **BASICS** -- self-defense techniques, freestyle techniques, forms (katas) etc. It also helps a student to visualize the directions from which an opponent can begin his attack. This directional reference can be further used to aid a student in selecting the proper direction of escape or retaliation when attacked. Thus, if we were to draw a line from 9 o'clock to 3 o'clock on this imaginary clock, any location forward of this horizontal line would be considered the front, any location to the rear of the same line would be considered the back (*see illustration*).

Side, left or right, refers to someone who is flanking you to your immediate left or right. Opponents or objects located to the left of a vertical line drawn from 12 o'clock to 6 o'clock would be considered to be on the left side, while anything to the right of the line would be the right side (*see illustration*).

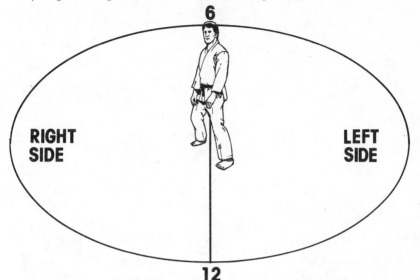

If you were to superimpose the vertical or 12 o'clock to 6 o'clock line on to the middle of the horizontal or 9 o'clock to 3 o'clock line (*see illustration*), you would not only have a cross, plus sign, or whatever, but an obvious division into four quarters. Therefore, if you were facing 12 o'clock and your opponent

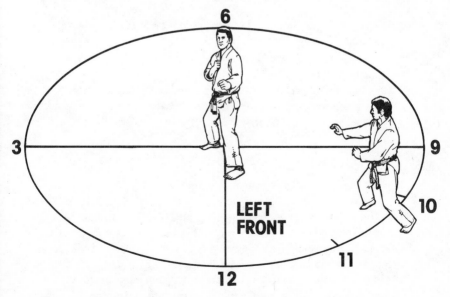

was at 10 o'clock, this would indicate a combination of both front and side. In this situation, he would be located at your left front quarter. A 2 o'clock, 4 o'clock or 7 o'clock location would place your opponent in the right front quarter, right back quarter, or left back quarter respectively.

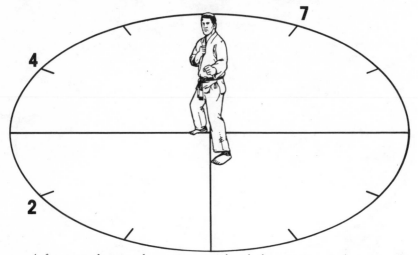

A front attack not only requires peripheral observance as to how an opponent is positioned in relation to you, but also as a gauge to question the effects that can stem from the attack. The following analytical process should assist you in using logic.

## 1. Direction and Location

    a. Where is your opponent located on the clock (using the "clock principle" as a visual aid)?

    b. How does this effect your line of defense (using 12 o'clock as the direction you are facing)?

    c. How does this effect your or your opponent's vulnerable areas? Is there easy access to targets and zone areas and what must you do to protect yourself or attack those that are on your opponent?

## 2. Stance

    a. What stance has your opponent assumed? Is it a wide, narrow, or a low stance?

    b. Does your opponent's stance effect his vulnerability or maneuverability?

    c. What position and posture has your opponent assumed and what have you done to match his?

    d. How does your opponent's position and posture effect the location of his weapons -- which hand or foot is forward (to the front) or back and how does the lead hand or foot in the forward position (to the front) correspond to, or effect the rear (back) hand or foot?

e. Will he initiate his attack from the forward (front) arm or leg, or from the rear (back) arm or leg?

f. How will the location of his weapons effect the direction of his weapons?

## 3. Distance

a. How does distance effect his choice of weapons? Will he render more kicks and leg techniques, or punches and arm techniques because of distance?

b. How will distance effect the method, path, dimension, and angle of your opponent's delivery?

c. How will his distance effect your strategy -- does it favor or hamper you?

d. How will your strategy be effected by his method, path, dimension, or angle of delivery?

Although this analytical process can increase your understanding of motion, let me now share a more in-depth and rewarding experience as I define the terms *method, path, dimension,* and *angle.*

*Method* is the underlying move(s) in which a block or strike can be executed. There are only two basic methods with which to execute a move -- linear (straight) and circular (curved). All the others are a variation of this.

**Straight**          **Circular**

When you are employing either of these methods, they follow certain *paths* that could be further sub-divided or classified as *horizontal, vertical,* or *diagonal* in nature. As these two methods follow *horizontal, vertical,* or *diagonal paths* our next sequential study of motion should entail *dimensions of travel.* *Dimensions of travel* are concerned with the *height, width,* and *depth of motion,* or the height, width and depth that can be created and controlled by motion. As your circular motion proceeds on a vertical overhead path you will inevitably question what dimensions of height your move should be confined

# ORGANIZATION CHART ON MOTION

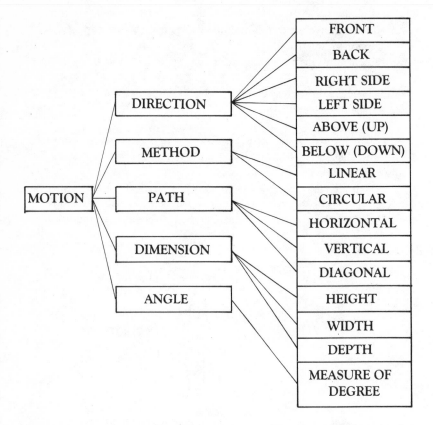

to. Too much height takes too much time, and prematurely telegraphs your action. This would naturally apply to the other dimensions of width and depth.

As you execute combinations of these aspects of motion, *angles of travel* should be considered. *Angles of travel* entail a more precise and acute viewpoint of direction. They describe *direction* as *degrees of measurement*. *Angles of travel* employ the "compass principle" where a student is made to visualize specific degrees on the compass to view motions of attack and defense. Observation would then specifically determine whether a diagonal kick was traveling on a 33 degree or 47 degree angle, etc. *Diagonal paths of travel* would then take on a more precise *direction of travel*. The organizational chart on motion (opposite page) should give you a better overall view of the composition of motion. Study it thoroughly.

Now that you have been appraised of the variety of avenues motion can take, let me discuss other contributing factors that can increase the effectiveness of motion. Increased effectiveness necessitates carrying an erect posture. An erect posture helps to maintain good balance. To enhance balance, you must learn to relax. Learning to relax enables you to increase your speed. Speed, however, must be coupled with accuracy. The development of accuracy teaches you how to properly use angles. Knowledge of the proper use of angles teaches you to be consistent in applying economy of motion. Economy of motion intensifies precisioned timing. Combine all of these contributing factors of motion and you will experience the ultimate in coordination. Coordination then magnifies focus, which in turn reinforces power. Power is generated even more when you add synchronization of the mind, breath, and body strength, body momentum, torque (rotating force), body alignment, back-up mass, gravitational marriage, and penetration to those listed above.

# CHAPTER 7
# DETERMINING
# YOUR CHOICE OF ACTION

Familiarizing yourself with the priorities of self-defense, the types of attacks you can encounter, and what motion entails, should enable you to logically analyze and dissect a technique. Technique dissection is an in-depth process of critical evaluation. As you analyze a specific technique, study is best begun by dividing your efforts into phases. *Phase I* of the analytical process requires that you commence with an *ideal* or *fixed* situation. This means that you are to select a combat situation that has been structured with a prescribed sequence of movements, and use this *ideal* technique as a basis to work from. In this phase, the term *ideal* implies that the situation is *fixed* and that the "*what if*" questions required in *Phase II* are not to be included in *Phase I*. Using the *ideal* technique or model situation as a reference point not only refers to the defensive moves you employ, but the anticipated reactions of your opponent as well. Technically then, it is the prescribed reactions of your opponent that completes the *ideal* technique. Therefore, the *ideal* techniques are built around seemingly inflexible and one dimensional assumptions for a good purpose; they provide us with a basis from which we may begin our analytical process, (like a control model in any reliable scientific experiment). Prescribed techniques applied to prescribed reactions are the keys that make a basic technique *ideal* or *fixed*.

In *Phase I*, structuring an *ideal* technique requires selecting a combat situation that you wish to analyze. Contained within the technique should be *fixed* moves of defense, offense, and the anticipated reactions that can stem from them. In deciding the predetermined moves and reactions, you should ask yourself the following questions:

1. What should I select in terms of the type of attack?
    a. Will it be for a grab, punch, kick, choke, etc.?
2. If I choose a punch;
    a. What direction is my opponent punching from?
        1) Is he approaching from 11, 2, 5, 7 o'clock, etc.?
    b. What hand is he using to punch with -- right or left?
    c. Is the hand he is striking with the lead or rear hand?

d. If he is using his lead, hand, did he step in with it -- that is did he step in with his right foot as he punched with his right hand?

e. What method is he using while he is executing the punch?
    1) Is the punch linear (straight)?
        a) Is it snapping or whipping?
        b) Is it thrusting?
    2) Is it circular (curved)?
        a) Is it a hammering type of punch, a roundhouse, hook, slice, rake, etc.?

f. What path is the punch following?
    1) Is it following a horizontal, vertical, or diagonal path?
        a) Is the punch traveling from outside/in or inside/out?
        b) Is the punch traveling from down/up or up/down?

g. What are the limits of the dimensions of travel?
    1) What is the extension of the height, width and depth of the punch?

h. What angle is the punch coming from?
    1) Is the technique meant to work on the inside or outside of the line of defense?
    2) Should the technique work above or below the angle of attack?


**NOTE:** These questions, as well as others, should be asked about a push, kick, etc. Once the main *idea* of a technique is structured, stick to the predetermined pattern and avoid "*what if*" questions at this phase.

The structuring of an *ideal* technique should further include *three points of view* -- your's, your opponent's, and the *bystander* who observes both you and your opponent. The need to analyze techniques from *three points of view* cannot be overemphasized. It is a strong concept in support of *Phase II* and adds flavor to the main idea of an *ideal* technique. It helps to understand other responses that can be triggered from your action. When you are avoiding, redirecting, stopping or immobilizing an opponent's actions and reactions, in using the analytical process, you should ask yourself the following questions:

1. Am I really covering or exposing my zones? The answer becomes apparent when you take your opponent's role. The inadequacies of your defense can be determined when his point of view is considered.

2. If exposure does exist, how many ways can your opponent counter you during that specific period? After exhausting all the possible ways in which you can be attacked or countered, you now have a deeper understanding of each of the newly discovered variables. Here is where the third point of view (that of a bystander) is valuable, since further answers can stem from taking this viewpoint.

3. Do you have a defense for your opponent's counters? It is conceivable that you may think of more counters than your opponent would when you assume the third point of view.
4. If so, how many answers are there and what are they? Once they are determined, familiarize yourself with them and practice them.
5. Is there one counter that can nullify the remaining possibilities? Learning these types of counters should take top priority.

Referring and relating to each of the *three points of view* is a must if you plan to work your basic technique toward an accurate application. As you learn to dissect each prescribed technique, you will also learn to automatically alter it according to your needs. When this occurs, you are now well into *Phase II.*

The above analytical process can become even more lengthy when *"what if"* questions are added. The tone of questioning in this instance slightly alters from *"what are they"* to *"what if"*. *"What if"* you do counter these additional variables, how would your opponent react? At this stage of *Phase II* you are programmed to thoroughly analyze probable variations to the model technique. Expected as well as unexpected opponent reactions are projected and evaluated. The principle here is that every movement has a consequence. Thus, the need to predict each consequence to the best of your knowledge, in a realistic situation, is imperative. Ideally, all consequential possibilities should be projected, evaluated and learned. To do so is to increase your ability to instinctively and randomly alter the basic technique and thus allow you the opportunity to determine your choice of action.

*Phase III* involves the actual application of your newly found alternatives to the original *ideal* or *fixed* technique. Knowing what can additionally happen within the framework of the *fixed* technique, teaches you how to apply your variable answers to a free and changing environment. This ultimate process of combat training can be learned by using what I term the *"formula/equation for combat"*. It took me an entire year to complete this *formula/equation.* I thought, experimented, analyzed, wrote, demonstrated, and revised my findings, and at times became totally frustrated. Although frustration compelled me to set this project aside on numerous occasions, I, nevertheless, pursued it to my satisfaction. Rewarding experiences taught me how to fill in the elements aligned with variable factors. It taught me how to arrive at logical solutions affecting a free and changing environment. It is this *formula/equation* process that I would like to share with you.

The following *formula/equation* should allow you a more conclusive basis for negotiating your alternate actions. The basic criteria is, to *any given base* whether it is a single move, or a series of movements, the following can be done:

1. You can *prefix* it -- add a move or moves before it.
2. You can *suffix* it -- add a move or moves after it.

3. You can *insert* -- add a simultaneous move with the already established sequence whereby this move can be used as;
   a. **A check:**
   1) **Pinning Check** -- where you use pressure against your opponent's weapons to nullify anticipated delivery of these weapons.
   2) **Positioned Check** -- where you place the hand or leg in a defense position or angle to minimize entry to your vital areas.
   b. **A simultaneous weapon.**
4. You can **re-arrange** it -- change the sequence of the moves.
5. You can **alter** it by changing the base move or moves as you:
   a. **Alter the weapon.**
   b. **Alter the target.**
   c. **Alter both the weapon and target.**
6. You can **adjust** your move(s) as a by-product of altering by:
   a. **Adjusting the range** (which effects depth).
   b. **Adjusting the angle of execution** (which effects width and height).
   c. **Adjusting both angle of execution and range.**
7. You can **regulate** your move(s) by:
   a. **Regulating the speed** of the action.
   b. **Regulating the force** of the action.
   c. **Regulating the force and speed** of the action.
   d. **Regulating the intent and speed** of the action (fake the move or use it as an offense).
8. You can **delete** -- exclude a move or moves from the sequence.

**NOTE:** *Altering, adjusting,* and *regulating* could be applied to single, or combination moves of a *prefix, suffix,* or *insert.*

It should be kept in mind that the methods outlined above are tools to aid you in exploring new ideas and creating new movement patterns. Answers to anticipated and unexpected reactions could conceivably cause you to create variables not yet envisioned. Once this occurs, creative dimensions aside from your original premise would then be developed. This can constitute a monumental task leading to perpetual questioning. The extent of your exploration naturally rests with you.

# CHAPTER 8
# SELF-DEFENSE TECHNIQUES

The **SELF-DEFENSE TECHNIQUES** described in this chapter have been carefully selected to acquaint you with the variety of *methods* and *principles* that *American Kenpo* offers. They have been dissected in detail to further increase your understanding of what each of the techniques contain, as well as the many principles that help to maximize your efforts. The techniques demonstrate simple as well as sophisticated methods of execution to allow you an opportunity to compare and examine the depth of their application. *Checks* of all types are demonstrated throughout this chapter to acquaint you with a number of methods of *deterring* or *preventing* counters.

To understand Kenpo techniques and how they function, you must have knowledge of physics. It is the study of our body and how our senses, through the use of mathematical laws, theories, concepts and principles of mass, speed, body alignment, angles, body momentum, gravitational marriage, rotating force (torque), focus, stability, power, penetration, etc., can make our body function intuitively. An in-depth study of these theories, concepts, and principles of physics will also reveal the sophisticated basics that are contained within embryonic basics.

Because Kenpo is an eclectic fighting science it accepts, adopts and applies other scientific disciplines to maximize its effectiveness. Knowledge of anatomy, physiology and geometry are logically entwined to insure practicality. Anatomy is viewed realistically with all avenues of logic considered. Scrutiny goes beyond just viewing vital areas, natural weapons and natural defenses. Proper formation of natural weapons is crucial along with the proper methods of executing them. The natural weapon, when it meets its target, must be properly formed and positioned if the likelihood of injury to the deliverer is to be minimized upon contact. Such incidentals as the thumb being properly tucked in, the wrist straight and fortified when meeting resistance, proper body alignment and direction (angle) during execution, add to the total effect.

Concepts of width zones, height zones, depth zones and obscure zones are welcome subjects of study. Out of these subjects stem principles of controlling the various zones, favorable use of zones, changing the angle of zones, etc. Like a chain reaction angle changes alter body positions which in turn introduces other related aspects. For example, the many aspects of body contouring, how to use body contouring to your advantage, the *fitting* of a natural weapon to its target, all come into focus. As these aspects converge, they add to the total picture. This does not include the additional benefits that await discovery.

Taking the above approaches increases our understanding and awareness of the movements of Kenpo to the point of developing excellent teachers. I firmly believe that we should teach all students to become teachers and not robots. With their learning skills deeply embedded and their understanding of how to teach others, a student learns refinement.

As you thoroughly study the various aspects of Kenpo techniques, remember to analyze them from at least *two points of view* -- your's and your opponent's. Naturally, if you understand your point of view, you will understand what to expect from your opponent. A *third point of view*, that of a bystander, is also recommended. Refer to **THREE POINTS OF VIEW** on page 1 of Volume I, and to page 98 of this Volume.

## BENEFITS AND POINTERS

**SELF-DEFENSE TECHNIQUES** are designed to cause an opponent to react in a specific way so that you can reasonably forecast the sequence of action that you are to follow. Creating reactionary positions on an opponent can effectively aid your sequential flow of anticipated action. Should your opponent respond as anticipated, you can take advantage of the situation by borrowing the force of his reaction to increase the effectiveness of your strike.

The *benefits* derived from **SELF-DEFENSE TECHNIQUES** are many. They teach:

1. Simple basics.
2. Combinations of basics.
3. The definitions of basics.
4. The many types of encounters that can occur.
5. To be aware of other methods outside of the ordinary.
6. That there are no two situations alike.
7. How and when to employ specific basics.
8. Where and when to accentuate power or force.
9. Flow, continuity, and economy of motion.
10. About action and reaction.
11. How to create anticipated reaction.
12. How to capitalize on reaction.
    a. go with the force
    b. use opposing force
13. Use of rhythmic changes.
14. Why one should employ back-up moves.

15. How to eliminate panic through the use of back-up moves.
16. Checking; how, where, when, and what to check.
17. How to adjust to height, width, and depth.
18. How to adjust to size, weight, and reach.
19. Principles, and how they can be tailored to each individual -- balance, body alignment, accuracy, body momentum, back-up-mass, gravitational marriage, focus, penetration, power, to name a few.
20. The use of variables within the formulation process.

Simple *pointers* to be heeded when you are employing **SELF-DEFENSE TECHNIQUES:**

1. When blocking outside of your opponent's arm, block at or above the elbow.
2. When blocking on the inside of your opponent's arm, block below the elbow.
3. To beat your opponent's action, meet it.
4. You can also have reaction beat action by moving your opponent's intended target (on your body) as the first order of priority.
5. Check your opponent's height and width zones by using a diagonal cross check.
6. To check your opponent's depth zone, jam and cause an injury.
7. To prevent your opponent from throwing or torquing, check his leverage points.
8. If you can force your opponent's head below his waist, you will keep his legs in check (prevent him from kicking).
9. To check an opponent's angle (line) of entry when L to R, or R to L:
    a. be on the line of entry.
    b. be on the inside of the line of entry.
    c. be over the line of entry.
    d. be on the weapon that can follow the angle of entry.
10. Be aware of the many axis points on your opponent's body so that you can always seek zones of sanctuary.
11. The alternatives in defending against a straight punch are:
    a. work on the inside of the arm.
    b. work on the outside of the arm.
    c. work on the outside and inside simultaneously.
    d. work under the arm.
    e. work over or above the arm.
12. Do not cause an orbital move to re-orbit back to you.

# REINFORCING INGREDIENTS

## SPEED

"He who hesitates meditates in a horizontal position", is a statement I use to imply the need for prompt action. It is a statement referring to terms related to *speed*. "Do it now", "I want it done this instant", "be prompt", "you'd better be fast", "be quick about it", "you must do it rapidly", "it depends upon the swiftness of your action", are terms that imply speed, or act to hasten velocity irrespective of direction or dimension. As we study these terms we learn that they are concepts related to distance and time. By definition speed is equal to the distance divided by the time ($s=d/t$) it takes to act or move.

Speed, however, goes beyond the definitions described. Like the Eskimo who uses a number of terms to describe the types of snow, we, too, must distinguish and categorize speed to make it meaningful to the Kenpo enthusiast. There are *three categories of speed -- perceptual, mental,* and *physical* (body performance). However, although categorized separately in order to analyze what speed entails, they nevertheless function as one.

*Perceptual speed* is the *quickness of the senses* to monitor the stimulus that it receives, determine the meaning of the stimulus, and to swiftly convey the perceived information to the brain so that mental speed can parlay the response. To the Kenpoist, it is the feel or smell of trouble, a sound that detects trouble, a sign or gesture that suggests trouble, seeing the incoming strike, the inviting opening, or the opportunity to attack or counterattack. Speed of this type can be increased by maintaining alertness and by conditioning the senses to harmonize with environmental awareness (see Volume I, Chapter 11).

*Mental speed* is the *quickness of the mind* to select appropriate movements to effectively deal with the perceived stimulus. Speed of this type, however, can only be increased by practicing the various aspects of Kenpo techniques on a regular basis. This involves learning the techniques to a point of total familiarity and instinctive response (mental speed) in nullifying the threat. As you broaden your knowledge of alternatives and can conceptualize the random answers that exist in your subconscious mind, your instinctive response (mental speed) increases proportionately when it is triggered by the perceived stimulus.

*Physical speed* (body performance) is the *promptness of physical movement --* the fluency in response to the perceived stimulus. In Kenpo, it is the speed of the actual execution of a technique. Speed of this type can be increased through stretching, body conditioning, and other proper methods of training. Stretching exercises help to increase elasticity which automatically develops reach. Body conditioning prevents fatigue and allows body speed to function for longer periods of time. Knowledge of the principle of economy of motion also contributes to speed. It avoids erroneous angles, and teaches you how to administer your strength (power) in obtaining the most for your efforts in the shortest possible time. This principle (1) stresses the importance of being relaxed when striking -- tensing only at the moment of impact, (2) makes one aware that time is crucial, (3) uses movements that follow direct angles and paths, (4) eliminates telegraphing unless used as a means of deceptive strategy; teaches (5) continuity, flow, and *motion rhythm* (a topic that needs further elaboration), (6) to respond from wherever your natural weapons are located at the time of combat (point of origin), no matter what your, or your opponent's, body position may be at the time; (7) target accessibility and the distance, or range, that exists between your opponent's targets and your natural weapons, (8) the time it will take to get to the target of your choice, and (9) to also consider the speed of your opponent's action or reaction when analyzing economy of motion. A concluding note -- while body speed often enhances power, it is without doubt not the root of power. Synchronization of body mass and speed are two of the major ingredients that add to creating power.

# POWER

POWER is the culmination of several principles -- the sum total of which maximizes one's expenditure of energy. To obtain it, one must add all ingredients associated with economy of motion (proper body alignment, the following of direct angles and paths, etc.) so as to enhance speed. You must also add a mixture of torque (rotating force), body momentum (horizontal momentum through the use of shuffles; and diagonal or vertical momentum utilizing gravitational marriage), and deliver your strike and all movements from their point of origin. Every action must be simultaneously coordinated to bring about focus at the exact moment of contact.

It has been stated that when mass is coupled with velocity power increases proportionately. While this may be true, we should examine the term mass as it relates to power. Many refer to the mass of a natural weapon used to strike a selected target. In fact, it is the general consensus of martial artists that the mass of the natural weapon employed is what creates power at the time of target impact. While this statement may be true in part, it is not the total answer. As explained in Volume IV, POWER is the magnification of force aided by concentrated focus. Its capacity is proportionate to the physical strength, force, or energy exerted, in addition to the speed rendered. *Focus* is the concentration of mind, body, breath and strength culminating at the exact instant while blocking or striking a specific target. What does all of this mean? Is it the mass of the natural weapon as it strikes the target that creates the force needed to increase power, or is it the entire mass of the body in synchronization with the natural weapon that maximizes power? The answer is obvious, the entire body must be in focus with the target in order to fully utilize mass. Yes, the mass of the natural weapon does start off independent of body mass, but at a given point, all culminate upon impact. Therefore, it is not only the mass of the natural weapon, but the added mass of your body that synchronizes at the point of contact. Mass takes in the entire body and not just a portion of it.

Other contributing factors that lend to power depend on the *angle of incidence, surface concentration,* and *penetration. Angle of incidence* refers to your weapon making contact with your target on a perpendicular angle (right angle to each other) that will render the greatest effect. *Surface concentration* is an important aspect to consider if increased injury is contemplated. It is concerned with the impact force between weapon and target and the resulting stresses that occur. It follows the principle of a pin or a nail where the surface of the natural weapon being used is as small an area as possible in order to have a more penetrating effect on the target. While surface injury is at a minimum, the internal effects are much greater. *Penetration* refers to the depth of your strike when making contact with your opponent's vital area (target). Strikes should be designed to terminate about an inch or two (depending upon the target) beyond the surface of the target. Since maximum velocity occurs between 70% and 80% of the way through your movement, it stands to reason that this is when impact should occur. The reasons for retrieving a strike rather than following through are two fold: It preserves your balance and economizes on your movements. After all, a strike that travels beyond the point intended is really no more than a wasted push. However, like in most facets of life there are always exceptions. If the strike is strategically used as a *check* after penetration (*lock-out punch*), it would not be considered *wasted.*

## SELECTED TECHNIQUES

As stated at the start of this chapter, the following **SELF-DEFENSE TECHNIQUES** have been carefully selected to acquaint you with the variety of *methods* and *principles* that *American Kenpo* offers. When studying these techniques, please examine the *meaning* of each of the principles, and make every effort to *understand them* thoroughly. You should then *practice* these principles diligently, and work them so that they become *spontaneous.* Accomplish this feat, and your physical skills will excel beyond expectation.

Like all instructional undertakings, comprehension is of primary importance. Therefore, I have showcased one of the techniques for you to analyze so that you, too, can duplicate the concept when you are working with other techniques. Please make note of the principles that have been highlighted by arrows and captions around each of the corresponding photos. Aside from enhancing your comprehension, it will make your practice sessions more enjoyable.

When delving into the following techniques, observe how they demonstrate simple, as well as sophisticated *methods of execution* that allow you the opportunity to compare and examine the depth of their application. Like the advice referencing *principles*, make every effort to learn these *methods of execution* thoroughly. Fathom how they work, how they may differ in appearance, but manage to apply identical principles. Learn to compare, experiment, refine, and alter them. Examine changing situations and learn to adapt these methods to each new situation. Study the *checks* that are combined with the various methods of execution. They will apprise you of the many ways which you can dually use your *checks* with your *strikes* to deter, or prevent counters from striking you.

To further your understanding, I have endeavored to include *notes* following each of the techniques. These notes are to familiarize you with the main *theme* or *premise*, and the **IDEAL PHASE** for which each technique was designed. The notes also contain **"WHAT IF"** factors. They suggest other variables that may occur within each of the techniques. Not to overlook **PHASE III,** the notes also include insights that allow you to **FORMULATE** according to prevailing circumstances.

The notes favorably extend beyond the norm. They acquaint you with the *basic coordination levels of movement, varying applications of timing and rhythm* (to your basic sequence of movements), and *how adhering to directives can further increase the efficiency of your movements.* Learning variations of a particular type of an attack, teaches you to build *spontaneity.* This, in turn, helps to *internalize concepts.* Internalized concepts cause newly acquired moves to also become *instinctive.* Consequently, as your spontaneous reactions increase with each new move, you become capable of randomly creating logical technique combinations of your own. Therefore, it is this creative ability that allows you the capability of *formulating* instinctively. As your creative experiences expand, you will discover that the same defense can be applied on the inside as well as the outside of your opponent's left of right arm with what will appear to be a *thoughtless response.* Through practice and experience you will also learn that inserting the normal flow of one technique with that of another, in part, or in total, becomes the automatic by-product of spontaneity. Your spontaneous reactions readily adjust to changing circumstances. Develop these inherent qualities and you will discover instinct to be routine.

It is my fervent hope that a detailed study of the notes will foster knowledge that cultivates useful variables in each of the techniques. Also, I hope that you learn to discern elements that create variables, be able to identify all types of attacks, and to suitably apply *master key moves* that will aid you in terminating each and every threat. Perhaps what I have just stated may sound idealistic, but nevertheless, learn to work with partners of varying heights, size, reach, etc. With each workout, consider all practical alternatives relating to each of the variables. Be aware of exposed targets; yours as well as your opponent's. Learn all beneficial methods to protect your exposed targets, as well as the many ways in which you can take advantage of your opponent's targets. Learn to observe your partner, but more importantly, use your imagination visualize the *attitude, reaction,* and *response* of a real, aggressive opponent, and the effects that can be anticipated. *Remedy* each anticipated response accordingly. In the creation of each of your anticipated variables, alter the *directions* of your opponent's attack (between 4:30 and 1:30), or from whatever direction you may prefer. This in turn will alter your *lines of attack*, and increase your knowledge of how to cope with each changing situation. Learn to do the above and you are well on your way to discovering the merits of **TAILORING.**

As you read all explanations associated with each of the techniques, try to absorb as much of the details as possible. May I assure you that the details were not written to confuse you, but to increase your awareness of the many particulars that exist. Needless to say, when you learn the details competently, spontaneity, and instinct becomes habitual.

The **SELF-DEFENSE TECHNIQUES** of my choosing are as follows:

1. **Lone Kimono** - left front lapel grab (O-7)
2. **Crossed Twigs** - rear two hand grab to the wrist (B-15)
3. **Five Swords** - inside of right punch (O-9)
4. **Entwined Maces** - right and left punch with opponent's left leg forward (2nd BRWN-21)
5. **Detour from Doom** - right front roundhouse kick (G-4)
6. **Dance of Darkness** - right front kick followed by a right punch (2nd BRWN-4)
7. **Grip of Death** - left flank headlock (O-12)
8. **Obstructing the Storm** - right overhead club attack (P-19)
9. **Raining Lance** - right front overhead knife attack (3rd BRWN-7)
10. **Capturing the Rod** - right front pistol (2nd BRWN-18)

Please take special notice of the following descriptions. I have condensed some of the basic terms to keep the captions simple. For example, I have excluded the word *"stance"* when referring to a horse, right neutral bow, 45 degree cat, etc. However, while many of my sentences are brief, they do convey the major point(s) desired. On the other hand, I have included short, but descriptive phrases in parentheses, to heighten your understanding. The *clock principle* is used throughout to help you pinpoint direction.

# 1. LONE KIMONO (Front left hand lapel grab)

1.  Standing naturally, step back toward 6 o'clock with your left foot into a right neutral bow (facing 12:00). Simultaneously pin your opponent's left hand to your chest with your left hand as you deliver a right upward forearm strike against your opponent's left elbow (slightly above the joint) to cause an elbow break or sprain. See photos 1 through 3.
2.  Then circle your right arm over and down (counter clockwise) with a diagonal inward-downward strike against your opponent's left forearm. Finish with your right palm up "with" your left hand checking high. Make sure that your opponent's left arm is driven down and diagonally to your left. View photos 4 and 5.
3.  Your opponent is now coming down and toward 7:00. *Round the corner* as you strike with a right snapping outward handsword to the right side of your opponent's neck. Keep your left hand checking in the *neutral zone*. Examine photo 6.
4.  Right front crossover, covering out between 7:00 and 8:00 o'clock. Observe photos 7 and 8.

**NOTE:** Although beginning students are not required to do more than step 3, intermediate students are required to continue the sequence by executing step 4. Examine the relevance of this precautionary maneuver.

 1

 2

 3

 4

 5

 6

 7

 8

# PRINCIPLES PERTAINING TO LONE KIMONO

1.  1. Point of Origin
    2. Depth of Action
       a. Create Distance
    3. Body Rotation
       a. Fulcrum Point
    4. Minimize Target
    5. Pinning Check
       a. Anchor Elbow
       b. Rotate Opponent's Hand (Arm) on the Pin.
    6. Angle of Disturbance
    7. Angle of Cancellation
    8. Stabilize Your Base
       a. Keep Knees Flexible
       b. Settle
    9. Body Alignment
    10. Angle of Execution
    11. Counter Manipulation
2.  1. Circular Rotation
       a. Preparatory Torque
    2. Angle of Execution
       a. Use of "X" Pattern
    3. Torque
    4. Anchor Elbow
    5. Frictional Pull
    6. Positional Check
    7. Fulcrum Point
       a. At Opponent's Wrist
3.  1. Rounding the Corners
    2. Angle of Execution
       a. Complimentary Angle
    3. Borrowed Force
       a. Use of Opponent's Reaction to Increase the Force of Yo
          Action.
    4. Angle of Incidence
    5. Rebounding Check
    6. Tracking
    7. Positional Check
4.  1. Angle of Departure
    2. Positional Depth of Action
    3. Angle of Protection

# SPECIAL INSTRUCTIONS

A study of principles (see opposite page) is an important learning tool. As you will notice (on page 112), the very first move of **LONE KIMONO** contains eleven (11) principles. Moves two (2), and three (3) indicate seven (7) principles, and move four (4) lists three (3). What does all of this mean, you may ask? The answer is simple. In the case of movement number one (1) there are eleven principles that occur during this single count. It must be remembered that although there is only a single count, you are simultaneously doing several bits of action. When you step back, you are to move back from your *point of origin*. That is, you are not to move forward, to the side, or raise your head before dropping back. You are to simply drop back from the very position (spot) you were in. Dropping back (*depth of action*), creates distance (a very good ally). While you are moving, your body *rotates* using your right foot as a *fulcrum point*. This in turn *minimizes the vulnerable targets* on your body. With this action, your left hand is used to execute a *pinning check*. What this means is that while your left hand pins your opponent's left hand to your chest, this action also keeps your opponent's left hand in check -- thus preventing his hand from striking you. To get the maximum benefit from this pin, you are advised to *anchor your left elbow*. To help secure the grab, cover your ribs, and control your opponent's arm by *rotating it*. The pinning of your opponent's arm while stepping back will cause an *angle of disturbance* as well as an *angle of cancellation*. All of this occurs as your left foot plants, with your *knees kept flexible to help settle* your body and *stabilize your base*. Stepping back places you in balance as you disturb your opponent's balance momentarily canceling his retaliatory actions. All of these *checks* help to place your *body in proper alignment* to insure a more suitable *angle of execution*, and be more effective when you are employing *counter manipulation*. All three, *body alignment*, *angle of execution*, and *counter manipulation*, triggered by *body rotation* and *torque* from your right arm create phenomenal results.

The following pages illustrates how you should condition your thinking regarding *principles*. Reconstruct similar examples and you will find them to be rewarding when you are practicing **SELF-DEFENSE TECHNIQUES.**

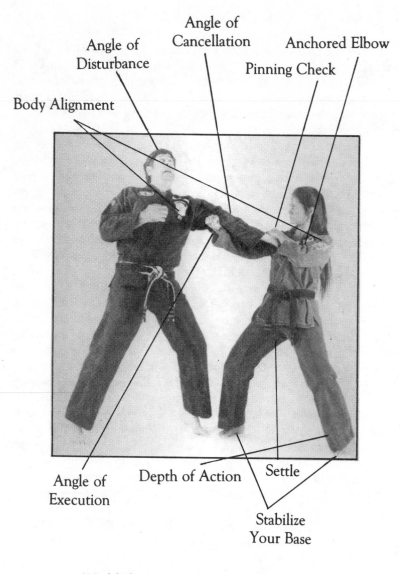

Angle of
Cancellation

Angle of
Disturbance

Anchored Elbow

Pinning Check

Body Alignment

Angle of
Execution

Depth of Action

Settle

Stabilize
Your Base

Highlights of Some of the Principles
that Occur on the First Move

Angle of Cancelation

Control of
Height Zone

Angle of Execution

Positional Check

Anchored Elbow

A Few of the Principles that Occur
on the Second Move (with some Additions).

Angle of Incidence

Borrowed Force

Angle of
Execution

Positional Check

A Few of the Principles that Occur
on the Third Move

# NOTES FOR LONE KIMONO:

1. **NAME:** The name of this technique stems from two sources; "*lone*", referring to "*single*", and "*kimono*", relating to "*robe*" or "*shirt*". The fact that the attack is a *single hand grab to the shirt* is the reason for the technique being named *Lone Kimono*.

2. **THEME:** This technique was devised because of the common practice of many Americans to grab their opponents by the shirt. As you will discover, similar attacks may be countered by similar principles, and/or slight alterations of these principles.

3. **THE ATTACK:** The **IDEAL PHASE** of this technique begins with your opponent to the front. He steps forward with his left foot as he grabs the left side of your shirt with his left hand, and then proceeds to extend his arm in an effort to push you back. Study these additional **WHAT IF** factors:

   a. Your opponent pulls you toward him.
   b. Your opponent follows his left grab with a right punch.
   c. Your opponent attempts to jerk you forward and down.
   d. You cannot step back.

4. Do not overlook the experience of the one who is grabbing you.

5. A hand that grabs is momentarily a dead hand. Take every advantage of the opportunities that grabs offer you.

6. "A multiplication sign (X) is nothing more than a plus sign (+) turned on its side." See how this saying applies to this technique.

7. Build spontaneity by having your partner vary his attacks: left lapel grab, or left hair grab. Respond to these variables with either a right middle knuckle fist to his left arm pit, or a left upward forearm strike to his left elbow. This method of practice will help you to internalize the concept that *similar attacks* using *different paths* may be countered by *similar responses* using *different angles of execution.*

## 2. CROSSED TWIGS (Rear two-hand grab to wrists)

1. With your feet together, and your opponent grabbing both of your wrists from the rear, countergrab both of your opponent's wrists (right to right and left to left) as you step to 1 o'clock with your left foot into a left neutral bow. This should help disturb your opponent's balance, especially if you pull forward and down with your left arm. (Do not overlook pulling with your right arm.) See photos 1 and 2.

2. Pivot clockwise facing 7 o'clock (still maintaining the wrist grabs) as you cross your opponent's arms (right over left). In the process have your right elbow strike diagonally (from down/up) and outward to your opponent's right jaw hinge, and continue the flow of your right arm to pull your opponent's right arm down. Have your left hand, which is grabbing your opponent's left wrist, pull down and below the level of your buttocks. See photos 3 through 7.

3. Release your right grasp, and loop your right arm counter-clockwise, as it now becomes a right inward overhead elbow strike down to the upper spine of your opponent. View photos 8 and 9.

4. Release your left grasp. Now, with both your right and left hands free, execute two downward heel palm strikes to your opponent's left kidney and left ribcage (left hand to left kidney and right hand to left ribcage). Take note of photos 10 and 11.

5. As you grab and pinch your opponent's kidney and ribs stabilize your opponent's body with both of your arms, and simultaneously deliver a left knee strike to your opponent's right ribcage. Observe photo 12.
6. Replant your left foot toward 1 o'clock into a right neutral bow (still facing your opponent), and execute a right front crossover, and cover out twice toward 1 o'clock. Refer to photos 13 through 15.

9

10

11

12

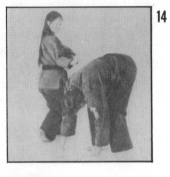

13

14

15

# NOTES FOR CROSSED TWIGS

1. **NAME:** The name of this technique stems from the symbolic meaning of *twigs*, which refers to the *arms*. Your opponent's *arms* (*twigs*) are *crossed* during the course of your defensive action, thus the name *Crossed Twigs*.

2. **THEME:** This technique was designed to appraise you of the merits of counter grabbing your opponent, pulling him off balance, and, while unbalanced, crossing his arms to prevent him from retaliating. Accomplishing this momentary tie-up allows you the freedom to counter your opponent at will. This technique also acquaints you with the principle of *compounding* where, during the course of crossing your opponent's arms, you can logically and comfortably insert an elbow strike to your opponent's jaw. This is done *within* the normal sequential flow of your action.

3. **THE ATTACK:** The **IDEAL PHASE** begins with your opponent grabbing both of your wrists from the rear in an effort to restrain you. Study the following **WHAT IF** factors:

   a. Your opponent pulls you toward him.
   b. Your opponent forces you to move forward.
   c. Your opponent cross grabs you.
   d. Your opponent grabs your elbows instead.
   e. You cannot step forward.
   f. Your are butted up against a corner.

4. Do not overlook the strength of your opponent.

5. Compare this technique with all others, and consider how creating an *angleof disturbance* works in your favor.

6. List the *types* of *body momentum* and the number of *times* they occur during the course of this technique.

7. Examine the value of tightening your circular paths of action. See how it not only helps your *timing*, but how it places your moves in proper "*sync*", helping you to *increase the speed and force* of your strikes.

8. See the value of *timing* when applying the principle of *"sandwiching"*.

9. Practice counter grabbing your opponent's wrists, and get the proper *"feel"* of its *application.* Proper application induces proper and successful *manipulation.*

10. Scrutinize the need for a precise angle when employing the principle of *angle of incidence.*

## PRINCIPLES PERTAINING TO CROSSED TWIGS

1. 1. Point of Origin
   2. Angle of Deviation
   3. Matching Counter
   4. Settle
      a. Drop
   5. Angle of Disturbance
      a. Yank
   6. Control of Height Zone
2. 1. Body Rotation
      a. Fulcrum Point
   2. Counter Manipulation
   3. Obscure Zone
   4. Body Contour
   5. Borrowed Force
   6. Angle of Incidence
   7. Continuity of Motion
   8. Angle of Cancellation
   9. Stabilize Your Base
   10. Control of Height Zone
3. 1. Continued Angle of Cancellation
      a. Yank
   2. Control Maintenance
      a. Continue Controlling Height Zone
   3. Continuity of Motion
   4. Circular Rotation
   5. Angle of Execution
   6. Angle of Incidence
   7. Fitting
   8. Positional Check

4. 1. Control Release
   2. Angles of Execution
   3. Angles of Contact
      a. With Both Hands
   4. Twin Factor
      a. Upper/Lower Case
5. 1. Fitting
      a. Via Grab and Squeeze
   2. Sandwiching
   3. Anchor
      a. Both Elbows
   4. Stabilize Your Base
      a. Settling on One Leg
      b. Bend and Drop
   5. Double Check
6. 1. Recover
      a. To Point of Origin
   2. Angle of Departure
   3. Positional Depth of Action
   4. Angle of Protection

# 3. **FIVE SWORDS** (Front right step through roundhouse punch)

1. While standing naturally, have your right foot step forward into a right neutral bow (facing 12 o'clock), checking the inside of your opponent's right knee with your right knee. In the process, execute a right inward block to the inside of your opponent's right wrist, while using your left hand to check high. See photos 1 and 2.

2. Immediately strike to the right side of your opponent's neck with a right outward handsword. Observe photo 3.

3. Pivot into a right forward bow (facing 12:00) as you execute a left horizontal finger thrust (palm down) to your opponent's eyes while your right hand cocks to your right hip (fist clenched and palm up). Examine photo 4.

4. Having caused your opponent's head to move away from you, pivot into a right neutral bow as you strike with a right uppercut punch to the stomach. In the process your left hand becomes a *cocking check* (it is guarding horizontally, palm down near your right bicep). View photos 5 and 6.

5. With your opponent now bent over, immediately have your left foot slide counter clockwise (to 4 o'clock) into a right forward bow as your left outward handsword strikes to the left side of your opponent's neck. Your right hand acts as a check for potential danger from your opponent's left arm during your circular wind-up for your next move. Refer to photos 7 and 8.
6. Without hesitation, and while pivoting into a right neutral bow, have your left hand hook around the left side of your opponent's neck, pulling his head down, followed by a right inward handsword to the back of your opponent's neck. See photo 9.
7. Right front crossover, covering out between 4:00 and 5:00. Observe photos 10 and 11.

# NOTES FOR FIVE SWORDS

1. **NAME:** This technique was originally developed where all *five counts* were executed as *handswords*. Because of the undeveloped state of the natural weapons of most beginning students the weapons were altered with the name unchanged.

2. **THEME:** In this technique, *environment* dictates that you cannot move back, nor is it feasible for you to move to the outside of your opponent's right punch. With your choice of action limited, you must learn to move *forward* and to the *inside* of his punch. Your timing is of utmost importance. You must time your action so that your block meets his right arm with success while contemplating checking the left arm of your opponent. This action will delay the use of your opponent's left arm, and give yourself ample time to strike him.

3. **THE ATTACK:** The **IDEAL PHASE** of this technique begins with your opponent located to the front. He steps forward with his right foot as he delivers a right roundhouse punch toward your face. Study these other possible factors:

   a. Your opponent throws a right straight punch.
   b. Your opponent pushes with his right hand.
   c. Your opponent throws a right uppercut punch.
   d. Your opponent executes a left straight punch.
   e. Your opponent pushes you with his left hand prior to punching with his right.
   f. Your opponent precedes his punch with a right kick.
   g. Your opponent attacks with a right roundhouse club attack.
   h. Your opponent thrusts a knife.
   i. The environment allows you to back up on your initial move.

4. Practice *formulating* this technique against a right/left punch combination.

5. Avoid the habit of blinking your eyes while executing your sequence of movements and you will be amazed by the increase in both the accuracy and the effectiveness of your techniques.

6. The habit of blinking should also be avoided when taking the role of the aggressor. You will reach new levels of self-defense training when this habit is eliminated.

7. Your right outward handsword (on the second move) should be executed at an angle that will cancel your opponent's height, width, and depth zones.

8. Vary both weapons and targets when practicing your basic technique sequence. Learn to tailor your weapons to the particular individual who is attacking you. As an example, convert the left horizontal finger thrust (third move) to a heel palm strike.

9. Your ability to buckle your opponent's right leg with your right leg will be one of the determining factors that can delay the use of his right hand.

## PRINCIPLES PERTAINING TO FIVE SWORDS

1. 1. Point of Origin
   2. Economy of Motion
   3. Body Alignment
   4. Directional Harmony
   5. Back-Up- Mass
   6. Body Momentum
   7. Angle of Entry
   8. Angle of Deviation
   9. Depth of Penetration
   10. Obscure Zone
   11. Buckle
   12. Angle of Disturbance
   13. Angle of Cancellation
       a. Partial
   14. Body Rotation
   15. Angles of Delivery
       a. Both Hands
   11. Angles of Contact
       a. Both Hands
   12. Anchor
       a. Both Elbows
   13. Borrowed Force
   14. Double Check
2. 1. Continuity of Motion
   2. Rounding the Corners
   3. Body Rotation
       a. Partial

4. Torque
   a. Right Hand
5. Angle of Execution
6. Borrowed Force
7. Angle of Incidence
8. Anchor
   a. Elbow
9. Defensive- Offense
10. Hugging Check

3. 1. Body Rotation
   2. Angle of Execution
   3. Contouring
   4. Body Alignment
   5. Back-Up- Mass
   6. Torque
   7. Angle of Incidence
   8. Depth of Penetration
      a. Greater Reach
   9. Bracing Angle
      a. Left Foot Using Ground

4. 1. Body Rotation
   2. Torque
      a. Right Fist
   3. Opposing Forces
   4. Borrowed Force
   5. Angle of Incidence
   6. Stabilize Your Base
      a. Settle
   7. Cocking Check
      a. Left Arm

5. 1. Angle of Deviation
   2. Up The Circle
      a. Shortens The Distance
   3. Opposing Forces
   4. Borrowed Force
   5. Angle of Incidence
   6. Knife Effect
   7. Sliding Check

6. 1. Borrowed Force
   2. Contour
      a. Fitting
      b. Hook Shape
   3. Body Rotation
   4. Anchor
      a. Left Elbow

5. Circular Rotation
   a. Right Arm
6. Marriage of Gravity
7. Angle of Execution
8. Angle of Incidence
9. Knife Effect
10. Settle
    a. Stabilize Your Base
11. Positional Check
    a. Left Hand and Arm
7. 1. Angle of Departure
2. Positional Depth of Action
3. Angle of Protection

**4. ENTWINED MACES** (Left and right punch with opponent's left leg forward)

1. With feet together, drop back with your left foot into a right neutral bow as your right hand loops a figure eight, first with a right inward on the outside of your opponent's left punch and a right extended outward on the outside of opponent's right punch. View photos 1 through 4.
2. Immediately shuffle forward as you deliver a left vertical punch to your opponent's face. Simultaneous with this action, have your right extended outward drop, and hook (or guide) your opponent's right arm down and to your right while shifting into a right forward bow. Inspect photo 5.
3. While in place, pivot into a right neutral bow as you deliver a right thrusting chop to your opponent's left jugular vein, switching your left hand as a check against your opponent's right arm. Refer to photo 6 and 7.
4. Follow-up with a left rear crossover, and deliver a right stiff leg reverse bow to buckle your opponent's left leg from the inside out while simultaneously delivering a right downward hammerfist to your opponent's groin (your left hand is guarding in front of your chest). Study photos 8 through 10.

1

2

3

4

5

6

7

8

5. From a right reverse bow pivot clockwise (in place) into a right front twist stance as your left hand assumes a positional check. Simultaneously deliver a right vertical outward back knuckle rake against the right side of your opponent's nose to break it. Immediately follow-up with a left heel of palm strike to opponent's sternum, and a left knee strike to your opponent's groin (cocking your right clenched fist to your right ear). Notice photos 11 through 14.

6. Plant your left foot back to 6 o'clock, checking with your left hand, and (from your right hand cocked position) immediately drop your body mass (*gravitational marriage*) as you deliver a right thrusting, chopping hammerfist strike to your opponent's left collar bone (could seek other targets if more advantageous). See photo 15.
7. Immediately execute a left rear crossover and a right back kick to opponent's solar plexus. View photos 16 through 18.
8. Right front crossover, and cover out toward 7 o'clock. Observe photos 19 and 20.

# NOTES FOR ENTWINED MACES

1. **NAME:** The name of this technique stems from the action that transpires between defender and aggressor. In this particular technique the aggressor's punches (clenched fists) resemble attacking *maces*. The method of countering these punches entails weaving in between them. As you view the action, the defensive maneuvers literally *entwine* the attacking *maces* during the initial activity, thus the name *Entwined Maces*.

2. **THEME:** This technique apprises you of what can be done against combination punches when employing the *figure "8" pattern*. The value of the pattern rests with controlling the height and width zones of your opponent. Control of this nature prevents an opponent from an immediate response, thus his retaliatory efforts are hampered, at least for the moment. Use of the pattern also teaches you to utilize and increase the effectiveness of *borrowed force*. This technique also teaches you how to increase force when rotating into a twist stance. The generation of power is quite unexpected, and the results are devastating. A third method of generating power is to combine *body rotation* with *gravitational marriage*, thus, *grafting* two types of *body momentum*.

3. **THE ATTACK:** The **IDEAL PHASE** of this technique has your opponent attacking from the front as he executes a left and right punch with his left leg forward. Some of the **WHAT IF** factors that can occur are:

   a. Your opponent steps forward with his right leg.
   b. Your opponent lunges viciously with his punches.
   c. Your opponent changes the sequence of his punches--right, and then left.
   d. Your opponent employs round house punches instead.
   e. Your opponent delivers a straight left and a right uppercut.
   f. Your opponent tries to push you with both of his arms.

4. Instead of stepping back, shift your action to your left flank when executing your counters.

5. Strive to perfect the force that is generated when your shuffle, right hooking hand, and left vertical punch are in "*sync*". Total synchronization is the key.

6.   Examine the merits of a reverse bow and arrow stance as a *buckle* and as a method of exposing your opponent's groin.

7.   Practice striking when rotating into your twist stance. Perfect this method of generating power.

## PRINCIPLES PERTAINING TO ENTWINED MACES

1. 1.   Point of Origin
   2.   Circular Rotation
   3.   Body Rotation
   4.   Start of "X" Pattern
        a. Start of Figure "8"
   5.   Settle
        a. Stabilize Your Base
   6.   Completion of "X" Pattern
        a. Complete Figure "8"
2. 1.   Angle of Cancellation
        a. Control of Height and Width Zones
   2.   Body Momentum
        a. Push-Drag Shuffle
   3.   Body Alignment
   4.   Back-Up-Mass
   5.   Synchronized Weapon
        a. Left Fist
   6.   Bracing Angle
        a. Via Right Forward Bow
        b. Using the Ground for Support
   7.   Control Maintenance
3. 1.   Body Rotation
   2.   Torque
        a. Right Arm
   3.   Angle of Delivery
   4.   Angle of Incidence
   5.   Knife Effect
   6.   Pinning Check
        a. Left Hand
   7.   Settle
        a. Stabilize Your Base

4. 1. Control Maintenance
      a. Left Hand
   2. Angle of Deviation
   3. Circular Rotation
      a. Right Arm
   4. Depth of Penetration
   5. Synchronization
      a. Of Weapon and Stance
   6. Buckle
   7. Angle of Disturbance
   8. Angle of Delivery
   9. Angle of Incidence
   10. Positional Check
      a. Left Hand
5. 1. Body Rotation
   2. Synchronization of Weapon
      a. "With"
   3. Angle of Contact
      a. Right Fist
   4. Body Contour
   5. Angle of Delivery
      a. Left Heel Palm
   6. Angle of Incidence
   7. Needling
      a. Left Knee
   8. Weapon Alignment
   9. Angle of Delivery
   10. Angle of Incidence
   11. Position Cock
      a. Via Circular Rotation
6. 1. Body Rotation
   2. Depth of Action
      a. Left Foot to Point of Origin
   3. Positional Check
      a. Left Hand
   4. Torque
      a. Right Arm
   5. Gravitational Marriage
   6. Synchronized Timing
      a. Of Weapon and Plant

7. Path of Action
   a. Right Fist
8. Depth of Penetration
9. Angle of Contact
10. Settle
    a. Stabilize Your Base
7. 1. Body Momentum
      a. Via Left rear crossover
   2. Body Alignment
      a. Via Angle of Entry
   3. Angle of Delivery
   4. Angle of Incidence
8. 1. Angle of Departure
   2. Positional Depth of Action
   3. Angle of Protection

## 5. DETOUR FROM DOOM  (Front right roundhouse kick)

1.  While in a right neutral bow, quickly shift your left foot (up the circle) to 4 o'clock into a right 45 degree cat stance. Simultaneously deliver a left downward block to the inside of your opponent's right leg as you thrust a right vertical punch to your opponent's face. Observe photos 1 through 3.
2.  From your right 45 degree cat stance, deliver a right front snapping ball kick to your opponent's groin. See photo 4.
3.  Plant your right foot toward 10 o'clock into a right neutral bow as you simultaneously execute a left vertical punch to your opponent's solar plexus with a right horizontal forearm check on top of your opponent's arms (photo 5).

4. Deliver a right back knuckle strike to your opponent's stomach as your left foot shifts to 3 o'clock into a right neutral bow. Examine photos 6 and 7.
5. Immediately have your left hand hook downward on the back of your opponent's neck as you continue circling your right arm counterclockwise, and deliver a right inward overhead hammerfist to the back of your opponent's neck. Take note of photos 8 and 9.
6. Right front crossover and cover out toward 3 o'clock. Follow photos 10 and 11.

# NOTES FOR DETOUR FROM DOOM

1.  **NAME:** The name stems from the *maneuver* selected to get you *out of the line of* your opponent's *right kick*. Consequently, your left foot shifting **up the circle** is a maneuver that allows you the capability of *detouring* from the path of your opponent's kick. This action eliminates the threat of *doom* and devastation. Accordingly, with the proper maneuver, you can competently *detour from doom.*

2.  **THEME:** This technique teaches you the merits of **moving up the circle** to get you out of the line of attack, as well as how you can extend the range of your right vertical punch. The timing of the foot maneuver and the punch is crucial in maximizing your power. Timed with precision, *body momentum* becomes the chief contributor to the sum total of your force. This technique is also unique in that the first action triggers the second action (your right ball kick to your opponent's groin), as if they were consolidated as one. Although precise timing gives you the illusion of consolidation, the two moves are, nonetheless, separate. The *shifting of your feet,* and *gravitational marriage* are repeated principles that help enhance the use of *body momentum.*

3.  **THE ATTACK:** The **IDEAL PHASE** of this technique is a front right step-through roundhouse kick to your stomach. Study the following **WHAT IF** factors:

    a. Your opponent's kick is delivered to your head.
    b. Your opponent fakes a low kick to your groin and then delivers a roundhouse kick to your head.
    c. Your opponent's roundhouse kick is followed by an overhead handsword strike to the left side of your neck.
    d. Your opponent's roundhouse kick is followed by a thrusting left punch.
    e. Their is a wall to your immediate right that restricts your movements.
    f. Formulate beyond what the technique suggests.

4.  Practice delivering the right back knuckle strike to your opponent's face. **Alter targets** to help broaden your experience.

5.  After delivering your right inward overhead hammerfist to the back of your opponent's neck, flow into a left rear crossover and execute the concluding sequence of *Entwined Maces.*

6.  Learn how to *graft techniques.* Acquaint yourself with how you can combine one technique (in full, or in part and have it flow (without

interruption) with that of another (in full, or in part).

7.   Familiarize yourself with *altering* and *tailoring*.

# PRINCIPLES PERTAINING TO DETOUR FROM DOOM

1.   1.   Point of Origin
     2.   Body Rotation
     3.   Angle of Deviation
     4.   Up the Circle
          a. Increase Range
     5.   "With"
          a. Synchronization of Weapon, Block, and Stance
     6.   Body Alignment
     7.   Angles of Delivery
          a. Left (Block)
          b. Right Fist (Strike)
     8.   Angle of Incidence
          a. Right Fist
     9.   Settle
          a. On Left Leg
          b. Stabilize Your Base
2.   1.   Point of Origin
     2.   Angle of Delivery
          a. Right Ball of Foot
     3.   Angle of Incidence
     4.   Stabilize Your Base
3.   1.   Depth of Action
     2.   Gravitational Marriage
     3.   "With"
          a. Synchronization of Weapon and Stance
     4.   Angle of Delivery
          a. Left Fist
     5.   Angle of Incidence
     6.   Positional Check
          a. Left Arm
     7.   Stabilize Your Base
4.   1.   Point of Origin
     2.   Angle of Deviation
     3.   Up the Circle
          a. With Left Foot
          b. To 3 O'clock
     4    "With"
          a. Synchronization of Weapon and Stance
     5.   Angle of Delivery
          a. Right Back Knuckle

147

   6. Angle of Incidence
   7. Positional Check
      a. Left Hand
   8. Stabilize Your Base
5. 1. Contour
      a. Shape of Crane
      b. Your Left Hand to Opponent's Neck
   2. Gravitational Marriage
   3. Alternating Timing
      a. Of Left Hand and Right Handsword
   4. Anchor
      a. Left Elbow
   5. Circular Rotation
      a. Right Arm
   6. Angle of Delivery
      a. Right Handsword
   7. Angle of Incidence
   8. Anchor
      a. Right Elbow
   9. Pinning Check
      a. Right Forearm
   10. Positional Check
      a. Left Hand
   11. Stabilize Your Base
6. 1. Angle of Departure
   2. Positional Depths of Action
   3. Angle of Protection

## 6. DANCE OF DARKNESS (Right front kick followed by right punch)

1. While standing in a right fighting stance, and as your opponent kicks, drop back with your right foot to 5 o'clock into a left front twist stance as you execute a right downward parry to slide along and deflect his right kick (from 11:00 to 5:00). Your left hand is now up in the neutral zone. See photos 1 through 3.

2. As your opponent now attempts to punch execute a double parry (left inward and right outward) to the outside of his right arm, and with this action, step out and to your right to 10:30 with your right leg and settle into a right neutral bow stance. Study photos 4 through 6.

3. Continue to step around and behind of your opponent with your left leg into a left neutral bow stance, and cock your hands (cup and saucer) to your left hip, now pivot clockwise into a right close kneel stance as you execute a right back-knuckle strike "with" a left vertical punch to his spine (your right hand is on the bottom to act as a check if needed). Refer to photos 7 and 8.

4.  Immediately grab (with your left hand) and vigorously pull your opponent's right shoulder down, as you simultaneously thrust a right vertical back knuckle strike to his right temple (your left hand is still checking at or below his right shoulder). This action creates opposing force, which in turn aids in using borrowed force. Examine photos 9 and 10.

5.  These next moves are timed almost simultaneously. Drop your right punching hand into a small counterclockwise loop, and execute a right two-finger hook to the right eye of your opponent, and without hesitation, circle your left checking hand around and under your right arm so that it follows and slides along the outer right side of your arm to act as a guide so that you can slip in an eye poke to the same eye. The initial hook is done as you sweep your opponent's right leg, and your last poke is timed so that it hits at the same time you plant out of the sweep into a left front crossover. Refer to photos 11 and 12.

6.  From your twist stance, pivot clockwise, and execute a right spinning leg sweep to buckle the back of your opponent's right leg. Your leg hits his leg bent and then straightens to accentuate the force. View photos 13 and 14.

7. Right from the sweep (your opponent should now be down with his head pointing toward 10:00 o'clock), execute a right step through "*retarded ball kick*" to the jaw of your opponent. Scrutinize photos 15 through 17.
8. Plant your right foot (gauging leg) and execute a left side thrusting knife-edge kick to your opponent's face. Inspect photos 18 and 19.
9. With your left foot still in the air, left front crossover (photo 20) and proceed with the routine cover out toward 4:30 o'clock.

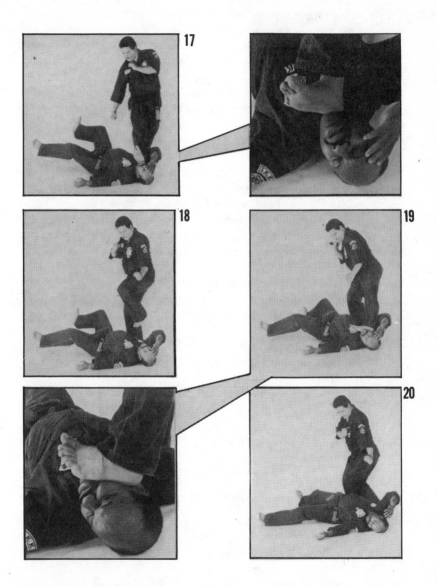

## NOTES FOR DANCE OF DARKNESS

1. **NAME:** The name of this technique refers to the *dance-like* appearance of the sequence used to counter your opponent's attack. Since application of the technique can cause temporary blindness, the term *darkness* was symbolically used to describe the possible occurrence of sightlessness. Thus, the name *Dance of Darkness* refers to the counter moves (*dance*) that can cause blindness (*darkness*).

2. **THEME:** This technique was designed to teach you how to strategically retreat before advancing to complete the sequence. The counters used to foil the attack employ an array of principles worthy of study. With little effort, and with positive results, you can employ the *double factor* to *deflect* and *check* the angle of your opponent's strike. The technique further stresses the importance of proper hand positions, when striking, to insure that defense is incorporated with your offense. *Tracking*, *object obscurity*, *fitting* and combination *leg sweeps* are other aspects that add to your vocabulary of motion. The experiences derived from this technique will help increase your knowledge of the inner workings of *counter manipulation.*

3. **THE ATTACK:** In the **IDEAL PHASE** of this technique your opponent is to the front in a left fighting stance. He then executes a right front kick followed by a right punch. Study the following **WHAT IF** factors:

   a. Your opponent executes a right kick followed by an overhead chop.
   b. Your opponent executes a right punch followed by a right kick.
   c. Your opponent executes a left front kick followed by a right kick.
   d. Your opponent executes a right front kick followed by a left punch.
   e. Your opponent executes a left front kick followed by a left punch.

4. When employing the *double factor*, take special note of the importance of checking *at* the elbow, and *not below* it when working on the *outside of* your opponent's arm.

5. Perfect the *timing of your sweep*. Develop the full potential of its use.

6. Differentiate between *opposing force* and *borrowed force*, and determine which of the two aids the other.

7. Examine how *tracking* insures accuracy, and how it can be applied in other techniques.

8. Study the merits of *fitting* when executing your *retarded ball kick* to your opponent's *jaw*.

9. Familiarize yourself with the sub-categories of *contouring*. Be able to make the distinction and define them.

## PRINCIPLES PERTAINING TO DANCE OF DARKNESS

1. 1. Point of Origin
   2. Positional Depth of Action
      a. Right Foot
   3. Angle of Deviation
   4. Angle of Deflection
      a. Right Hand
   5. Positional Check
      a. Left Hand
   6. Settle
      a. Stabilize Your Base
2. 1. Angle of Deviation
      a. Right Foot
   2. Depth of Action
   3. Double Factor
      a. Left and Right Hands
   4. Angles of Deflection
      a. Two Angles are Created
   5. Positional Checks
      a. Left and Right Hands
   6. Stabilize Your Base
3. 1. Depth of Action
      a. Left Foot
   2. Positional Cocks
      A. Left and Right Hands
   3. Synchronization
      a. Of Body Rotation and Gravitational Marriage
   4. "With"
      a. Simultaneous Strikes in "sync" *with* Body Rotation and Gravitational Marriage

5. Angles of Delivery
   a. Left and Right Fists
6. Angles of Incidence
7. Positional Check
   a. Right Forearm
8. Stabilize Your Base

4. 1. Contact Manipulation
   a. Left Hand Grab
2. Control of Height Zone
3. Body Alignment
4. Tracking
   a. Right Arm on Left
5. Object Obscurity
6. Angle of Delivery
7. Angle of Contact
8. Control Maintenance
   a. Left Hand
9. Stabilize Your Base

5. 1. Circular Rotation
   a. Right Arm
2. Chronological Order of Alternating Action
   a. Right Two-Finger Hook
   b. Left Leg Sweep
   c. Left Two- Finger Poke
3. Tracking
   a. Left Hand Using Right Arm
4. Object Obscurity
5. "With"
   a. Synchronization of Left Poke *with* planting of Left Foot
6. Positional Check
   a. Right Arm

6. 1. Body Rotation
   a. 320° Degrees
2. Depth of Action
3. Buckle
   a. With Right Leg
4. Guidelining Check
   a. Right Arm
5. Pinning Check
   a. Left Arm
6. Bracing Angle
   a. Via Forward Bow
7. Stabilize Your Base

7. 1. Point of Origin
   2. Path of Execution
      a. Right Foot
   3. Angle of Delivery
   4. Angle of Incidence
      a. Right Ball of Foot
   5. Settle
      a. Stabilize Your Base on Left Leg
8. 1. Gauging Distance
   2. Fortify Your Base
   3. Body Rotation
      a. Pivot Point (Right Foot)
   4. Angle of Delivery
   5. Angle of Incidence
      a. Left Knife-edge of Foot
   6. Settle
      a. Stabilize Your Base on Right Leg
9. 1. Point of Origin
   2. Angle of Departure
   3. Positional Depth of Action
   4. Angle of Protection

## 7. GRIP OF DEATH (Left flank right arm headlock)

1.  With your opponent applying a headlock from your left side, step forward and to your left (to 10 o'clock) with your right foot into a right close kneel stance, while turning your head to the left, and tucking your chin against your chest. Simultaneously deliver a right hammerfist to your opponent's groin, and a left hammerfist to your opponent's left kidney. See photos 1 through 5.
2.  Circle your left arm over your opponent's right shoulder, and have the fingers of your left hand press under your opponent's nose (or, depending upon the circumstances, have your left hand grab your opponent's hair) to *fulcrum* your opponent's head back, using his shoulder as the fulcrum point. Scrutinize photos 6 through 9.

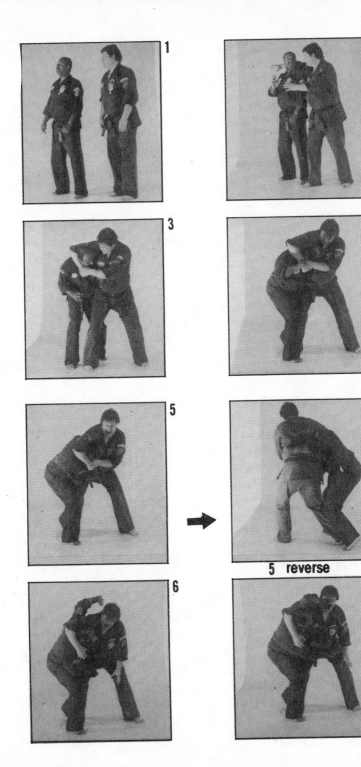

5 reverse

3. Immediately pivot into a left forward bow toward 6:00 to take advantage of *rotational force*. In the process, thrust a right heel palm strike to your opponent's chin. Simultaneously execute a left *sliding check* down your opponent's right arm, ending at the elbow. (Make sure that the head of your opponent, in either of the above cases, is arched and forced back and down to minimize your opponent's leverage.) Refer to photos 10 through 13.
4. Pivot back to a left neutral bow (no photo) and proceed with the routine left front crossover and double cover out between 10:00 and 11:00. Observe photos 14 and 15.

# NOTES FOR GRIP OF DEATH

1. **NAME:** The seriousness of this attack warrants the name. If properly employed the, *grip* can cause your *death*, thus the name *Grip of Death.*

2. **THEME:** The headlock is a very common attack used especially by people with wrestling experience. Internalize the importance of simultaneously responding with offensive and defensive principles. This simultaneous and spontaneous explosion will proportionately help you to protect yourself.

3. **THE ATTACK:** The **IDEAL PHASE** begins with your opponent at your left flank (9:00). Your opponent grabs your head, and pulls you into a side headlock. Consider these additional factors:

   a. Your opponent is stronger than you.
   b. Your opponent forces you to the ground.
   c. Your strikes have little effect.

4. Be sure to turn your head, and tuck your chin against your chest to prevent your opponent from cutting off your air supply.

5. Be sure to have your hammerfists strike their intended targets with accuracy.

6. *Borrow the force* of your opponent's initial pull when applying the headlock. This will magnify the damage rendered by your hammerfists, as well as increase the effect of your left knee buckling the back of your opponent's right knee.

7. Learn to *stabilize your base* on your first move to prevent your opponent from forcing you to the ground.

8. Analyze the *fulcrum* that is employed when prying your opponent's head back. See how you can obtain maximum leverage when nullifying his intentional or unintentional moves.

9. Increase the effect of your right heel palm strike (third move) by:

   a. employing the principle of *contouring*
   b. using proper *body alignment*
   c. using *back-up mass*
   d. *Fitting* your heel palm to his chin
   e. capitalizing on the merits of *penetration*

# PRINCIPLES PERTAINING TO GRIP OF DEATH

1. 1. Point of Origin
   2. Depth of Action
   3. Angle of Alignment
   4. Gravitational Check
      a. Left Knee
   5. Angle of Cancellation
      a. Check of Height Zone
   6. Positional Check
      a. Chin Tucked Against Chest
   7. Dual Strikes
      a. Left and Right Hammerfists
   8. Synchronized Action
      a. Of All Elements Above
   9. Solidify Your Base
2. 1. Circular Rotation
      a. Inside Out
      b. Under Nose
   2. Fulcrum
      a. Opponent's Shoulder
      b. Better Leverage
   3. Angle of Cancellation
      a. Control the Height Zone
   4. Angle of Disturbance
      a. Keep Opponent Off Balance
3. 1. Body Rotation
   2. Continued Angle of Disturbance
   3. Contour
      a. Your Ribcage
   4. Body Alignment
   5. Back-Up-Mass
   6. Angle of Delivery
   7. Angle of Incidence
   8. Bracing Angle
      a. Via Left Forward Bow
      b. Right Foot Using Ground for Support.
4. 1. Neutralize
      a. Equal Weight Distribution
   2. Angle of Departure
   3. Positional Depth of Action
   4. Angle of Protection

## 8. OBSTRUCTING THE STORM (Front right step through overhead club)

1. With your feet together, have your left foot step slightly forward and to your left on a 45° degree angle (first moving toward 11 o'clock, but ending facing 1 o'clock in a horse stance) as you cross your right wrist over your left wrist (upward cross block) to block your opponent's attacking hand at his right wrist, and at a level above your head and off of your right shoulder. Refer to photos 1 through 3.

2. Grab your opponent's right wrist with your right hand as your left foot steps forward to 1 o'clock ("*cat in and in front of* " your opponent's left leg) into a left neutral bow. Simultaneously strike your opponent's right elbow with your left forearm positioned vertically. Without hesitation, roll your left forearm horizontally, and force your opponent's right arm down as your right hand pulls in, down, and past your right hip. This action could force your opponent's head down, with the possibility of having his head strike your left knee. See photos 4 through 6.

1

2

3

4

5

6

3. Immediately deliver a right snapping knee strike to your opponent's head or chest while simultaneously pulling the club from out of your opponent's right hand. This is done without raising your body. View photos 7 and 8.

NOTE: To become familiar with **PHASE III,** the **FORMULA-TION PHASE,** you may employ one of two variations:

4. Plant your right foot forward while executing a whipping underhand club strike to your opponent's face (photo 9).

Or:

5. Pivot (inplace) into a left forward bow while simultaneously executing an underhand thrust with the end of the club to the right side of your opponent's face (photo 10).
6. You may replant your right foot to your *point of origin* (into your left neutral bow facing 1 o'clock) after completing step number 4, or pivot (inplace) into a left neutral bow after completing step number 5. In either case left front crossover (photo 11) and proceed with the routine cover out to 7 o'clock.

# NOTES FOR OBSTRUCTING THE STORM

1. **NAME:** *"Storm"* is a symbolic reference to a club attack. In this technique, you are not simply avoiding the club attack (*storm*), but are also *obstructing* its path of action.

2. **THEME:** Realizing that your opponent has a weapon that is extended, your response is to move out of the *line of attack.* However, deviating from the path of action is only one phase of the technique. You are to experience *obstructing* the threat, grabbing your opponent's wrist, and controlling his retaliatory efforts as well. This action may be necessary due to environmental limitations. If you were able to get to your opponent's right arm when it was still at the vertical apex of the circle, you could conceivably remain in the *line of attack,* and stop his action. However, that is an unrealistic approach if you did not wish to be countered unchecked. Disregard for zone control can prove disastrous. Therefore, visualize the circular plane that your opponent's body, arm, and club are travelling on with full force. Get off that plane and onto a new one. You can easily **"CATCH"** his arm if you get out of the *line of attack* and then *redirect* your body momentum onto a plane running from 7:30 to 1:30. If you execute your moves properly, the entire sequence can flow as one.

3. **THE ATTACK:** In the **IDEAL PHASE** of this technique the attack is from the front. Your opponent starts in a left fighting stance. He steps forward with his right foot as he executes a right overhead club attack. Some additional **WHAT IF** factors for study are:

    a. Your opponent does not step forward with his right foot.
    b. Your opponent changes the angle of his attack.
    c. Your opponent attacks from your left flank.
    d. There is a wall to your back.

4. Make sure that your head, shoulders, and legs are clear of the *line of attack.*

5. Look for the definition of *"catching"* in **Volume #3 of Infinite Insights into Kenpo.**

6. Investigate why your right hand is over your left hand in this *catch* and not vice-versa.

7. When practicing, be sure that your partner does not stop short of the mark with his club so that you can comfortably "do" the technique. You will not develop skill, nor confidence if your partner helps you to look good. Once you grasp the idea of the technique, have your partner increase the speed and power of his attack.

## PRINCIPLES PERTAINING TO OBSTRUCTING THE STORM

1.  1. Point of Origin
    2. Slight Angle of Deviation
    3. Depth of Action
    4. Out of Line of Attack
    5. Meet the Action
        a. With an *Open End Triangle*
    6. Borrowed Force
    7. Stabilize Your Base
2.  1. Control Manipulation
        a. Right Hand Grab
    2. Angle Change
        a. Left Foot
    3. Body Momentum
    4. Body Alignment
    5. Back-Up-Mass
    6. Opposing Forces
    7. Path of Action
        a. Squeegee Principle
    8. Angle of Delivery
    9. Angle of Incidence
    10. Continued Control Manipulation
        a. Via Rotation
3.  1. Point of Origin
    2. Angle of Delivery
    3. Angle of Incidence
    4. Settle
        a. On Left Leg
        b. Stabilize Your Base
4.  1. **Return to Point of Origin**
    2. Angle of Departure
    3. Positional Depth of Action
    4. Angle of Protection

## 9. RAINING LANCE (Front overhead step through knife attack)

1. While in a left neutral bow (or standing naturally), have your left foot shift forward and to your left (between 10 and 11 o'clock) into an off centered left neutral bow as your left hand (which is open) executes an inward parry on the outside of your opponent's right wrist (the hand being used to stab you). See photos 1 and 2.

2. With the right overhead knife attack still in motion, pivot to your right (into a horse) as your right hand assists your left hand in following the path and force of your opponent's knife hand. While still following the motion of the knife hand and without losing momentum, pivot to your left (into a left neutral bow), and jam the knife into your opponent's right thigh. Refer to photos 3 and 4.

3. Release your right hand as your left hand continues to jam and pin your opponent's right arm to his right leg to disallow the knife from being dislodged. Simultaneously deliver a right inward horizontal elbow strike to your opponent's sternum while shuffling forward (push-drag). Study photos 5 and 6.

4. Immediately switch hand positions by having your left hand, which was jamming and pressing your opponent's knife against his thigh, execute an outward reverse tiger's mouth (palm up) choke to your opponent's adam's apple. Simultaneously have your right hand (palm down) switch positions as it now continues to press the knife against your opponent's right thigh. View photos 7 and 8.

5. Again switch your hands so that your left forearm rolls and presses your opponent's right arm while your left hand grabs and squeezes your opponent's testicles. Simultaneously have your right hand (circle counterclockwise (palm down), hook, and pinch your opponent's eyes (crab hand pinch). Examine photos 9 and 10.

6. Allow space between your left foot and your opponent's right foot as your right hand hooks inside of your left arm and down to check opponent's right arm as your left hand slides up your opponent's body (after releasing opponent's testicles) to strike your opponent's throat with your left inner wrist. Take special note of photos 11 and 12.

7. Immediately switch your left inner wrist to a left hooking wrist (shape of the crane). As your right foot steps through to 11 o'clock, have your left forearm use your opponent's right shoulder as a fulcrum and leverage point, and force your opponent down and back. Immediately drop into a right wide kneel stance, and drive your opponent over your right knee to cause your opponent's back to break. Scrutinize photos 13 through 15.

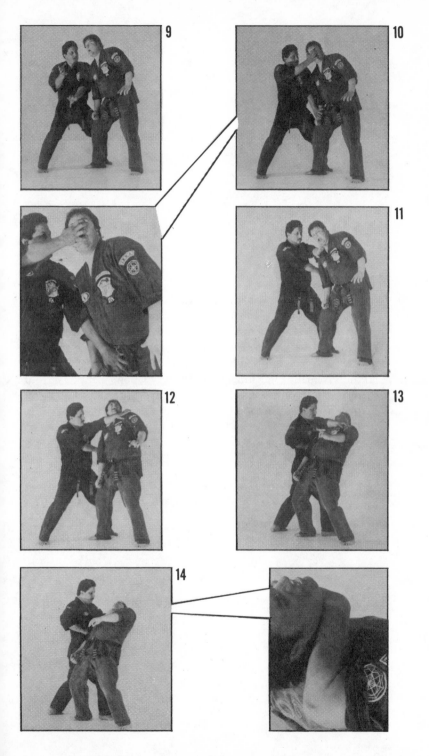

8. Almost simultaneous with the above move, circle your right arm in a counterclockwise manner, and deliver a right downward diagonal hammerfist strike across your opponent's throat, or left jugular. (Knife should be released at this point). View photos 16 and 17.
9. Deliver a left thrusting heel palm strike to your opponent's jaw (fingers pointed up) striking and forcing your opponent off of your right knee. Be sure to check your opponent's right shoulder with your right hand. See photos 18 and 19.
10. Right front crossover and cover out toward 6 o'clock. Refer to photos 20 and 21.

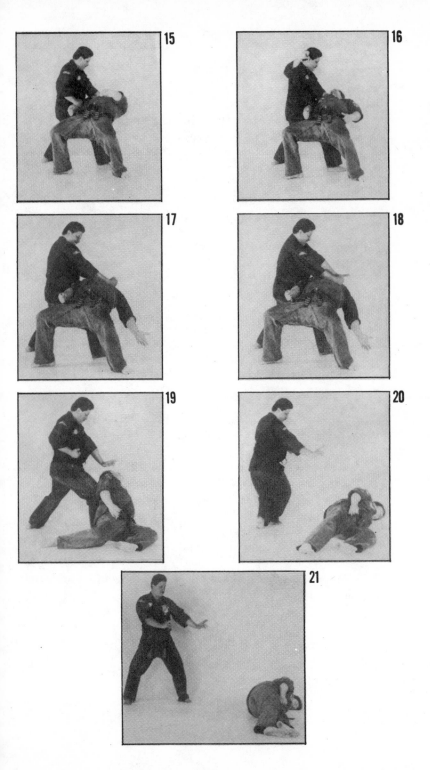

# NOTES FOR RAINING LANCE

1.  **NAME:** *Lance* is a symbolic term used to describe a *knife attack*. In this technique, the *knife* attack (*lance*) is executed in an overhead fashion. In its descent, the *knife* appears, like *rain*, to be coming out of the clouds. Thus the name *Raining Lance* describes the *knife* (*lance*) that descends like *rain*.

2.  **THEME:** This technique teaches the importance of how to get *out of the line of attack, and how to logically use your opponent's force to defeat himself*. Additional stress is placed on the need to control your opponent's knife. Control is accomplished by *jamming* the knife into your opponent's right thigh, and preventing it from being dislodged. The follow-up counters and alternating checks are also educational, adding greatly to your vocabulary of motion.

3.  **THE ATTACK:** The **IDEAL ATTACK** is a front overhead knife attack. During the execution of the attack, the knife is held in your opponent's right hand while stepping through with his right foot. The following are **WHAT IF** factors to consider:

    a. Your opponent follows a diagonal path (from right to left) when attacking in an overhead fashion with his right hand.
    b. Your opponent follows a diagonal path (from left to right) when attacking in an overhead fashion with his right hand.
    c. Your opponent steps forward with his left foot when attacking in an overhead fashion with his right hand.
    d. Your opponent steps forward with his left foot when attacking in an overhead fashion with his left hand.
    e. Your opponent fakes the attack a number of times before following through with his action.

4.  See the value of *contouring* as a check and as a guide to help increase the accuracy of your strikes.

5.  Make the distinction between *rolling checks* and *sliding checks* and 20 why they are considered methods of *contouring*.

6.  Review the importance of *synchronizing* your *step through foot maneuver with your strike*.

7. See how *fulcruming* gives you *leverage* to enhance the effectiveness of your technique, and why it, too, is considered a method of *contouring.*

8. See how *fitting* your left heel palm strike to your opponent's jaw enhances the effectiveness of your technique, and why it, too, is considered a method of *contouring.*

## PRINCIPLES PERTAINING TO RAINING LANCE

1. 1. Point of Origin
   2. Angle of Deviation
   3. Angle of Deflection
      a. Using Left Arm
   4. Partial Angle of Cancellation
   5. Partial Stabilizing of Base
2. 1. Added Assistance
      a. Right Hand Assisting Left
   2. Stance Transition
   3. Continued Path of Action
   4. Borrowed Force
      a. Assisting Knife to Opponent's Right Thigh
3. 1. Pinning Check
      a. Left Hand
   2. Body Momentum
      a. Push-Drag Shuffle
   3. Body Rotation
   4. Angle of Entry
      a. Right Inward Horizontal Elbow
   5. Angle of Incidence
      a. To Sternum
4. 1. Switch
      a. Hands
   2. Pinning Check
      a. Right Hand
   3. Angle of Entry
      a. Left Hand
   4. Vice-Like Maneuver
      a. Left Hand Choke to Adam's Apple

5. 1. Trade
   2. Rolling Check
      a. Left Forearm
   3. Pinning Check
      a. Left Forearm
   4. Vice-Like Maneuver
      a. Left Hand Squeeze to Testicles
   5. Angle of Entry
      a. Circular Path
   6. Angle of Contact
   7. Vice-Like Maneuver
      a. Right Pinch to Opponent's Eyes
6. 1. Angle of Deviation
      a. Left Foot to 10 O'clock
   2. Hooking Check
      a. Left Hand to Opponent's Right Arm
   3. Sliding Check
      a. Left Forearm
   4. Angle of Entry
      a. Via Contouring of Left Arm
   5. Angle of Contact
      a. Left Inner-Wrist to Throat
7. 1. Transformation
      a. Left Inner-Wrist to Left Hooking Wrist
   2. Body Momentum
      a. Via Step-Through With Right Foot
   3. Leveraging
      a. With Left Hooking Wrist Using Opponent's Right Shoulder
         as Fulcrum
   4. Angle of Disturbance
   5. Angle of Cancellation
   6. Change of Height Zone
      a. Drop into a Right Wide Kneel Stance
   7. Angle of Delivery
      a. Proper Guidance of Opponent's Back
   8. Angle of Incidence
      a. Opponent's Back to Your Right Knee
8. 1. Circular Rotation
      a. Right Arm
   2. Angle of Delivery
      a. Downward Diagonal
   3. Angle of Incidence
      a. Right Hammerfist to Throat

9. 1. Contouring
        a. Left Forearm Against Left Ribcage
        b. To Enhance Accuracy
    2. Angle of Delivery
        a. Left Arm
    3. Angle of Incidence
        a. Left Heel Palm to Jaw
    4. Follow- Through
        a. To Drop Opponent to the Ground
    5. Pinning Check
        a. Right Hand to Right Shoulder
10. 1. Angle of Departure
    2. Positional Depth of Action
    3. Angle of Protection

## 10. CAPTURING THE ROD
(Right front pistol against your chest a modified version of the IDEAL technique)

1. Standing naturally, with your hands down and to your sides, step forward and to your right toward 12 o'clock into a left front twist stance. This action is simultaneously done as you execute a left outward parry (close to your body) to deflect the *line of fire* of your opponent's gun. Be sure that your body pivots counterclockwise so that you face 9 o'clock. See photos 1 and 2.

2. Instantly follow your left hand parry with a left and right hand grab (palm down) to your opponent's left wrist and forearm respectively (photo 3).

3. With your right hand controlling your opponent's right wrist and gun from moving, execute a left two-finger snapping poke to your opponent's left or right eye (photo 4).

4. Immediately have your snapping left hand poke return to the underside of your opponent's right wrist (palm up) so that it can be used to assist your right hand in twisting your opponent's right wrist clockwise (photo 5).

5. Execute a right flapping elbow strike to the underside of your opponent's chin (photo 6).

   Drop back with your right foot toward 6 o'clock into a left neutral bow stance as your left and right hands twists your opponent's right wrist clockwise (photos 7 and 8). *Your life depends on your keeping the barrel of your opponent's gun pointed toward him at all times.*

   Yank the gun from your opponent's grip with your right hand while simultaneously executing a right front snap ball kick to your opponent's groin (photos 9 and 10). This should force the trigger finger of your opponent's right hand to do one of two things (if not both); break, and/or fire the gun.

6. As you plant your kicking right foot (forward toward 12 o'clock) into a right neutral bow stance, strike up with the butt of your opponent's gun in an arc so that your path of action travels diagonally out and upward to the jaw of your opponent. Make sure that your left hand is constantly checking your opponent's right arm during the course of action. Study photos 11 through 13.

7. Immediately execute a right inward downward diagonal strike to your opponent's left cheek bone followed by a right looping outward downward diagonal strike to the right side of your opponent's head or jaw as you follow through with your action so that the gun you're holding travels down, back, and past your right hip. When examining this action (photos 14 through 18), you will discover that the path of travel resembles the *figure "8" pattern*. Photo 18 illustrates the completion of your *figure "8" pattern* with your right foot stepping back toward 6 o'clock into a left neutral bow stance.

8. Without disturbing the flow of your action, execute a left front crossover as you grab the barrel of your opponent's gun with your left hand, and switch, by having your right hand grab the handle in the normal fashion so that you conclude this phase with a proper pistol grip. To complete the entire sequence of action, execute a right reverse step through as you position your left hand slightly below the gun as if in a guard position. (Do not let your left hand extend beyond the end of the barrel.) Free of your opponent, you now have the advantage of aiming his own gun at him. Study photos 19 and 20.

## NOTES FOR CAPTURING THE ROD

1. **NAME: Rod** is a symbolic term for *gun*. In the execution of this technique, the gun (*rod*) is grabbed (*captured*) to control the *line of fire* from crossing your body. In the control of the *line of fire*, the innocent bystander is also considered. Consequently, the name *Capturing the Rod* indicates that *control of the gun takes top priority* before follow-up moves can be executed to end the threat.

2. **THEME:** I have often stated, "It's not the gun that I am afraid of, but the bullet that's in it." In view of this statement, the primary aim of a defense against a gun is to keep the *line of fire* from crossing your body. This technique teaches you to *deflect and control the gun to permanently keep the line of fire away from you*. While the gun should be your primary concern, you are also encouraged to take every precaution to prevent your opponent's natural weapons from striking you. This technique offers you a number of opportunities to break, divert, distract, detain, restrain, and control your opponent's retaliatory efforts. Disarming your opponent, and then using his own gun to strike him with is highlighted in the technique.

3. **THE ATTACK:** In the **IDEAL PHASE** of this technique your opponent is in front of you with his right hand holding his gun against your chest. Some **WHAT IF** factors to study are:

    a. Your opponent has his left foot forward, with the gun in his right hand, held alongside of his right hip, and pointed at your chest.
    b. Your opponent is within distance, but slightly to your left with the gun in his left hand and pointed at your heart.
    c. Your opponent is within distance, to your left flank, with the gun in his right hand, and pointed to your head.

4. Practice this technique with your hands and arms in a raised position. See what modifications are needed to make the technique succeed from the raised position.

5. Do not fail to *compound* your technique. Stomps, buckles, strikes, etc. added to the uninterrupted flow of your action accent effectiveness and *sophistication*.

6. Practice diligently to gain accuracy with your finger pokes.

7. When twisting your opponent's right wrist to cause a sprain or break, learn to *condense the circular path* of that maneuver.

8. Perfect the timing of the yank and pull of the gun, simultaneous with your right kick. Execute the action with vigor.

9. When using the gun as a striking weapon, be aware of where the barrel of the gun is pointed at all times. Grab the cylinder if it's a revolver, or the hammer if its an automatic, to prevent the gun from firing by accident.

10. Keep a safe distance from your opponent, even after you are capable of using the gun on your opponent. Full control of the gun entails disallowing your opponent from getting it back.

## PRINCIPLES PERTAINING TO CAPTURING THE ROD

1. 1. Point of Origin
   2. Angle of Deflection
      a. Left Hand
   3. Body Rotation
   4. Depth of Action
      a. Right Foot
   5. Angle of Deviation
2. 1. Control
      a. Right Grab
   2. Stabilize Your Base
      a. Settle
3. 1. Continue Your Control
   2. Angle of Delivery
      a. Left Hand Poke
   3. Contour
      a. Use of Left Ribcage
      b. To Insure Accuracy
   4. Angle of Contact
      a. To Opponent's Eyes
4. 1. Control Assistance
      a. Left Hand Grab
   2. Control Manipulation
      a. Counterclockwise Wrist Twist
   3. Depth of Action
      a. Right Leg

4. Body Momentum
   a. Created by Depth of Action
   b. Timed With Wrist Twist
5. Body Rotation
   a. Timed With Depth of Action and Wrist Twist
   b. Increases the Effect of Wrist Twist

5. 1. In-place Transition
      a. Stance Change
   2. Counter Action
      a. Starting With Yank and Stance Change
      b. Can Cause Finger to Break or Gun to Fire
   3. Continued Counter Action
      a. Yank With Right Kick
   4. Borrowed Force
      a. Via Use of Opposing Force

6. 1. Gravitational Marriage
   2. Path of Travel
   3. Angle of Entry
   4. Angle of Incidence
      a. Butt of Gun to Jaw
   5. Pinning Check
      a. Left Hand

7. 1. Paths of Travel
      a. Figure "8" Pattern Using Butt of Gun
   2. Angles of Entry
      a. To Left Cheek Bone
      b. To Right Side of Head
   3. Angles of Incidence (Contact)
      a. To Left Cheek Bone
      b. To Right Side of Head
   4. Completed Path of Travel
      a. Have Right Hand With Gun Past Right Hip

8. 1. Return to Point of Origin
      a. Your Right Foot
   2. Angle of Departure
      a. Left Front Crossover
      b. With Transfer of Gun to Opposite Hand
   3. Positional Depth of Action

9. 1. Angle of Protection
   2. Positional Aim
      a. With Opponent's Gun

# CHAPTER 9
# FREESTYLE (SPARRING)

FREESTYLE (SPARRING) entails the *extemporaneous use of basic fundamentals.* These basic disciplines may employ (1) single moves; (2) simple combinations extracted from a **FORM, KATA,** or **SELF-DEFENSE TECHNIQUE;** (3) sophisticated combinations stemming from **SELF-DEFENSE TECHNIQUES;** or (4) strategic creations resulting from assorted combinations of (1), (2), and (3) via employing the *Formulation Stage* sighted in *Phase III.*

To benefit the novice, this chapter will commence with simple **FREE-STYLE (SPARRING) TECHNIQUES.** The illustrations will then graduate to combinations stemming from, and confirming the usefulness of, the *Formulation Stage.* However, to understand **FREESTYLE (SPARRING),** in its entirety, I consider it best that we first review the many ingredients that add to the total makeup of **FREESTYLE.**

As previously stated, **SELF-DEFENSE TECHNIQUES** and **FREE-STYLE TECHNIQUES** share identical functions, elements, facets, and principles. Consequently, it is not uncommon to witness disciplines, functions, elements, and facets, from each of the categories, overlap each other. Although selected priorities may vary between the two categories, it is also likely that circumstance may cause priorities to vary (independently) within each of the categories. I, therefore, would like to recall, review, and highlight the many ingredients discussed in Volumes I through IV that are referred to collectively as **FREESTYLE (SPARRING) TECHNIQUES.**

If you wish to construct a home or building, with every assurance that it will be built precisely and concretely, it is highly recommended that you hire an architect. As a professional he is expected to draft blue prints to insure that the contractors follow an authenticated and organized plan. As they perform their responsibilities they learn to function systematically to get the most from their efforts. The point being, most facets of life need a base an organized plan that can structure and formulate the system that is being studied. Following such a format not only lends to greater understanding, but insures ensuing logical and progressive paths.

As stressed in Volume I, Chapter 3, **FREESTYLE** is divided into two categories **TOURNAMENT** and **STREET.** Each have merit and it would be best that we review and compare these two categories. **TOURNAMENT**

**FREESTYLE** is further divided into "**NO** or **LIGHT CONTACT**" and "**FULL CONTACT** or **KNOCKOUT**" tournaments. More recently the term **KICK BOXING** has been identified with **KNOCKOUT** tournaments. Regardless of the types of tournaments discussed, they all fall under the **SPORTS** phase of the Martial Arts. The only other difference worth mentioning is that "**NO** or **LIGHT CONTACT**" tournaments are the **AMATEUR** division and "**FULL CONTACT** or **KNOCKOUT**" tournaments are the **PROFESSIONAL** division of the Martial Arts.

Of the **AMATEUR** and **PROFESSIONAL** divisions, the latter offers greater pugilistic value. It provides experiences that are more closely related to realistic predicaments. Both, however, employ rules that restrict, limit, and hamper street versatility.

Let us now refer to Volume I and explore the reasons that can cause restrictions and limitations. The section on Preparatory Considerations found in Chapter 11 provides us with some of the answers for both tournament competition, and street combat.

## ACCEPTANCE

The first topic of discussion is **ACCEPTANCE**. This consideration implies that you should **ACCEPT** the possibility of physical confrontation. Likewise, when you register to enter a tournament, as a contestant, you must **ACCEPT** the fact that you will encounter problems. "What from?" you ask? Those situations that can originate from **ENVIRONMENT**, the second Preparatory Consideration.

## ENVIRONMENT

Remember, **ENVIRONMENT** encompasses those elements that are *around you, on you,* or *in you; prior, during,* or *after* a tournament; or when you are involved in street combat. Close examination of this statement, therefore, reveals to us several possible occurrences. Examination of those elements that are *around you* should bring to the surface the following questions and thoughts if you were ever a tournament competitor:

1. Are there established rules?
2. What are the rules?
3. Are they familiar to you?
4. Are these rules contrary to what you expected?
5. Are you prepared to enter if contrary to what you expected?
6. Can you quickly adjust to them?
7. Do the rules require that you wear a specific uniform?
8. Will you be allowed to wear what you have?
9. If not, what effect will this have on you entering the contest?

10. If not permitted to enter, will you be reimbursed for your entry fee?
11. Can you convert your entry fee to a spectator ticket?
12. Will the tournament promoter be willing to reimburse you for the difference?
13. Are you willing to absorb the cost of a wasted trip?
14. Do the rules require safety gear?
15. What types of safety gear are acceptable?
    a. Cup and supporter?
    b. Hand and foot pads?
    c. Mouth piece?
    d. Others?
16. If not acceptable, do you have money to buy what is required?
17. Can you borrow someone else's gear?
18. Again, if you do not have the required protective gear will you be allowed to enter?
19. If not, the same problems can arise as those listed above.
20. Consideration must also be given to officials, for they can be a major concern.
21. Do you know the officials?
22. Do you know of their qualifications?
23. What are they known to look for during freestyle or form (kata) competition?
24. If you are entered in freestyle (sparring), are you capable of keeping the majority of the officials on the side where you score the majority of your points?
25. Regarding your methods of execution, are they too fast to be seen and thus not be given a point?
26. Are your methods of execution in compliance with what the officials are accustomed to seeing when awarding their points?
27. If you are entered in form (kata), competition do you know what your officials favor hard or soft styles?
28. Armed with this knowledge, you would then have to decide whether you should alter your performance to comply with the tastes of what the majority of the officials favor.
29. It is a well known fact that officials are more inclined to lean toward their methods of execution and, therefore, base their decision on moves that resemble theirs. The criteria being that if they can identify, they can justify.
30. What happens when an official is confronted regarding his or her decision?
31. Will he or she stick to their decision, or can they easily be persuaded or intimidated by others?
32. Are the officials really paying attention to your performance, or are they being sidetracked by something or someone else?

33. What are your rights in the case of incompetent officials?
34. Can you call upon an arbitrator to render a fair and just decision?
35. Is the arbitrator thoroughly conversant with the rules?
36. Is the arbitrator interpreting the rules correctly?
37. Will the arbitrator be persuaded or intimidated by others?
38. If injured during Freestyle (sparring), will the tournament promoter provide adequate medical aid?
39. How qualified is the doctor, nurse, medic, etc?
40. If you are told by the medical aids that you cannot continue the match, will you be willing to accept this ruling, or will you protest?
41. What is the ring size?
42. Is the ring size something that you are accustomed to?
43. Is the ring area padded, or is the floor made of wood or cement?
44. Are you accustomed to competing on a wood or cement surface?

When mentioning those *elements that effect you* during tournament competition the following questions should be asked:

1. Does the gi (uniform) that you have on allow you freedom of movement?
2. Will you be able to kick or punch without restriction?
3. Is your gi (uniform) too big?
4. If so, can it hinder your performance?
5. Can your loose gi cause your opponent to grab it to control your actions?
6. If safety gear is required, how effective are you with it on?
7. Will wearing safety gear hinder your accuracy?
8. Is your equipment new or old?
9. If your equipment is old, will it constantly fall apart during the contest?
10. How does wearing equipment effect your control?

When referring to **ENVIRONMENTAL** elements that may be *within you* (internal aspects) during tournament competition, I direct you to the following questions:

1. What is the status of your health?
2. Are you ill?
3. How is your physical condition?
4. Are you in top shape?
5. Can you last without getting weary?
6. Will you run out of steam early?
7. What is your mental frame of mind (attitude)?
8. Are you intimidated by fighters who have a reputation?

9. Are you confident or afraid?
10. Will you allow fear to overcome your physical prowess?

As indicated above, **ENVIRONMENT** is an important consideration and, therefore, all of its influences must be taken into account. The list and statements above, however, just touch on those concerns. I heartily recommend that you take the time to think, analyze, and expound on what has been written. If you are prepared going into a tournament, the chances of victory will increase proportionately. This philosophy also applies on the street. Street combat needs sophisticated analysis far above the level of tournament competition.

# RANGE

**RANGE** should be your third consideration. How you gauge your **RANGE** determines whether you get hit, or more importantly whether you can reach, touch, score a point, hit, or hurt your opponent. Since **GAP, SPACE, AND DISTANCE** are counterparts of **RANGE**, and can work for or against you, I think it important that we investigate elements associated with **RANGE**. **RANGE** extends in all directions. If this is true, then **GAP, SPACE,** and **DISTANCE** also extend in all directions, and all dimensions should be taken into account. Thus, when we speak of closing the gap, bridging the gap, etc., we should automatically include the dimensions of *height, width,* and *depth.* In retrospect, all action bridging or separating **RANGE** can be classified as **DIMENSIONAL STAGES OF ACTION**.

# DIMENSIONAL STAGES OF ACTION

We often hear the terms, **GAP, SPACE, DISTANCE,** and **RANGE** used interchangeably, or viewed as having distinct and separate characteristics of their own. Let us first refer to the dictionary and see what it states. **GAP** is defined as being "a separation in space". **SPACE** is "a limited extent of one, two, or three dimensions: **DISTANCE, AREA, VOLUME**". **DISTANCE** is "the degree or amount of separation between two points". **RANGE** is "the space or extent included, covered, or used".

**DIMENSIONAL STAGES OF ACTION** include all of the above terms. These **DIMENSIONAL STAGES OF ACTION** view **SPACE** from *all aspects of height, width, depth,* and *direction,* and the **DISTANCES** that necessitate *maintaining, closing, controlling,* and *opening* the **GAP**. They sequentially employ *long, medium* and *close range* techniques while closing in on an opponent, or when covering out. Of interest is the staggering amount of alternatives that exist when employing close range techniques. These methods go beyond just strikes. They include various methods of contouring, locks and chokes, twists, dislocations and holds, as well as takedowns.

Gauging the **DISTANCE** between you and your opponent for purposes of defending or attacking requires a thorough study of the **DIMENSIONAL STAGES OF ACTION.** It involves *choice of weapon and target, arm and leg lengths* of both you and your opponent, *foot and body manuevers, speed and accuracy, action* (response) *and reaction* (counter response). Included are *intentional and unintentional* moves, *deceptive and deliberate* (committed) moves, *checking* (pressing, pinning, jamming, etc.,) *and nullifying* moves (while simultaneously striking). It further includes *controlling height, width, and depth zones, restricted* (environmental encumbrances, tournament rules,) *and unrestricted* (no rules, anything goes) moves, and *consideration of the extent of injury.* With the aforementioned information, one can then determine the **DIMENSIONAL STAGES** necessary to defend or attack with successful results.

With the knowledge that **DISTANCE** encompasses degrees of separation between you and your opponent(s), you should first become acquainted with the established number of *stages of* **RANGE,** within the "GAP", that are crucial in combat as well as tournament competition. Since **RANGE** refers to what one can do within the **SPACE** that comprises the "GAP", it can safely be said that there are basically *four stages of* **RANGE** that should concern you: *out of contact, within contact, contact penetration,* and *contact manipulation.* Out of contact **RANGE** refers to that stage of **DISTANCE** that places you out of the reach of your opponent, or vice versa. Unless foot and body maneuvers are used to bridge this **DISTANCE,** conditions are generally safe. *Within contact* RANGE means exactly what it implies the **DISTANCE** in which you or your opponent can be reached. Injury may not be as crucial, but damage, nonetheless, can occur. *Contact penetration* **RANGE** refers to the distance in which a weapon can effectively penetrate the depths of a target, thus magnifying the damage or injury that can occur to you or your opponent. *Contact manipulation* **RANGE** entails controlling an opponent, or vice versa. Injury can be administered through contouring, locks and chokes, twists, dislocations and holds, and takedowns. Obviously, these same techniques could be used to cause greater injury if either party wished to do so.

The *four stages of* **RANGE** mentioned above pertain to *depth.* **SPACE** that exists between low and high points relate to *height.* **SPACE** that separates points that flank each other (left to right) involves the dimension of *width.* Hence, *all* action selected to condense or extend **SPACE** (gap) that exists between points of *height, width,* and *depth* can be classified as being **DIMENSIONAL STAGES OF ACTION.**

# POSITION

**POSITION** is the fourth consideration. Whether competing at a tournament, or fighting on the street, the postural **POSITION(S)** that you employ should provide you with maximum protection and the ability to retaliate with spontaneity. Altering defensive postures allows you flexibility and mobility to go about your strategic tasks with continuity and purpose.

You may automatically be strategically **POSITIONED** when attacked. If so you are one step ahead. The discussion of **POSITION,** however, goes beyond just forming a proper posture or stance. **POSITION** also entails stationing yourself behind *environmental objects* that function as *defensive blockades.* Chairs, tables, stanchions, etc. are useful deterrents that can be employed to protect you.

Postural **POSITIONS** involve a number of factors. One of the components is the **STANCE,** or **STANCES,** you employ when switching or varying your postural **POSITIONS.** Knowledge, gained from my experiences, has taught me that **STANCES** can enhance mobility when attacking or defending. With proper weight distribution you can take swift action from your *"point of origin".* Your ability to spring forward or in reverse with rapidity, however, depends on your knowledge of how to *tailor* your **STANCES** to each situation. Street combat often requires that you place your feet closer together in order to allow you to spring forward, backward, or to the sides. Whatever the adjustments, *tailor* them to your needs. Remember to keep your knees bent and flexible.

Another component rests with your competence to appropriately **POSITION** and structure your hand, arm, and leg to each predicament. Subliminal defenses materialize when your hands, arms, and legs are suitably **POSITIONED.** They become built-in **BLOCKS** known as **POSITIONED BLOCKS.**

## POSITIONED BLOCKS

As stated in Volume III, Chapter 3, **POSITIONED BLOCKS** require the arms and/or legs to be placed in various height,width, and depth *positions* to thwart the efforts of an opponent. Proper arm and leg *positioning* can cause an offensive move to be blocked during delivery. Even though your opponent initiates the action, your *statuette position* can still cause a block. Such **POSITIONS** can be achieved by the correct placement of one arm, both arms or both arms and leg.

Depending upon the type of **STANCE** you assume, (whether one foot is back and the other forward), you will have a forward, rear arm, or both to **POSITION.** If both arms are used, one should be high, and the other low. They should not be at the same level at the same time. Your vital areas would, therefore, be exposed and vulnerable to attack. Refer to pages 48 to 49 in Volume III.

# ZONE THEORIES

As previously discussed in Chapter 4, an interesting fundamental relationship to **POSITION** can be found in the study of **ZONE THEORIES** (also refer to Volume IV, Chapter 6). To recapitulate, these theories are three dimensional studies of your and your opponent's anatomy, and the space surrounding him. I stress these theories to teach students of *American Kenpo* how to use their imagination to visually divide their opponent's body into vertical and horizontal **ZONES** (sections) as viewed from the front, side, or back. A student who is knowledgeable about its use can: (1) learn the ease with which he can penetrate an opponent's defense; (2) aid him in preventing an opponent from penetrating his defense; (3) how checking and/or placing controls on his opponent's body can thwart his opponent's retaliatory efforts (while simultaneously counterattacking his opponent); and (4) how a student's actions can be activated without his opponent ever realizing it. These theories are excellent educational tools that give students a more thorough understanding of the countless opportunities that exist in defending or attacking, and how to take advantage of them.

## REACTIONARY POSTURES AND POSITIONS

Another ingredient worthy of discussion involves **REACTIONARY POSTURES AND POSITIONS** that are often assumed *prior to, during,* or *after* combat. While a number of these **REACTIONARY POSTURES,** and **POSITIONS** result from strategically planned strikes, others stem from ignorance, or are learned from experience. Study of these **POSTURES** and **POSITIONS** are important since **TARGETS** alter with each change. Because of these **POSTURAL** and/or **POSITIONAL** changes, accessibility to **TARGET** areas can become a problem if one is not aware of the variety of retaliatory choices that exist. On the positive side, **TARGET** selection can become intuitive once this knowledge is learned. As a result, spot decisions become spontaneous, efficient, and effective. You must remember, however, that your choice of **NATURAL WEAPON** is determined by the **POSITION,** angle, or **DISTANCE** you are from your opponent. See Volume V, Chapter 5.

## MANEUVERS

The fifth consideration pertains to **MANEUVERS.** It is my conviction that priority should be granted to evasive **MANEUVERS.** This is especially true of beginners. Why allow yourself to be hit when unfamiliar with the rudiments of Kenpo? Seek **MANEUVERS** that *usher you away* from an assailant. Learn to establish **DISTANCE** first. As an ally, **DISTANCE** can curtail unwarranted difficulties. Defense first, offense second. There is no shame in pursuing the closest exit. Once the rudiments of Kenpo become instinctive, aggressiveness can then be expected and the extemporaneous use of Kenpo rudiments will seem commonplace.

To repeat Volume II, Chapter 7, **MANEUVERS** are unique strategic methods used to evade and/or attack an opponent. It involves traveling techniques and using an array of footwork patterns in addition to changing body **POSITIONS** and **POSTURES**. Employing these methods can aid you in increasing power, creating or decreasing **DISTANCE** (to your best advantage), be used preceding an attack, used simultaneously with an attack, or used after an attack. **MANEUVERS** are divided into two classifications **FOOT** and **BODY**.

## FOOT MANEUVERS

Movements or methods employing the legs to move about in any direction utilizing **STANCES** are classified as **FOOT MANEUVERS**. To state it differently, **FOOT MANEUVERS** are methods using the feet and legs to transport your body from one ground point to another while traveling in a multitude of directions. Examples of **FOOT MANEUVERS** are *step throughs*, *crossovers*, *twist outs*, *shuffles* (step-drag, drag-step, push-drag, pull-drag), *jumps*, and *dives*. Associated with **FOOT MANUEVERS** are **BODY MANEUVERS**. For more detailed information please refer to Volume II, Chapter 7.

## BODY MANEUVERS

**BODY MANEUVERS** are methods that are employed to move the upper torso in any direction to either avoid being struck, or to enhance an offensive action. When exclusively employed, it is your body that is in motion and not your feet. In other words, the upper body moves while your feet remain on the same spot. When your feet are coordinated with the movements of your upper torso then you are combining both **FOOT** and **BODY MANEUVERS** to further enhance your action. Examples of **BODY MANEUVERS** are: *turning*, *riding*, *rolling*, *slipping*, *bobbing*, *weaving*, and *falling*.

## FEINTING

**FOOT** and **BODY MANEUVERS** can be effective by means of **FEINTING**. **FEINTING** is the use of deceptive gestures or **MANEUVERS** to lure, or cause your opponent to react. When an opponent reacts in accordance to your desired plan, it becomes a *set-up* which allows you the opportunity to follow-up with an effective response. The head, shoulders, arms, or legs all play an important role when **FEINTING**. Your **FEINT** can be implemented as a simple gesture, a pronounced action, or can employ a number of gestures (including facial gestures). When used consecutively, in a variety of time periods, **FEINTS** can create worthwhile results. Although **FEINTS** against the unskilled are not as necessary as against the skilled, they can cause a dramatic and favorable reaction to your combat strategy. Do not overlook the fact that *committed action* is what insures the usefulness of a **FEINT.**

In summary, although **FOOT AND BODY MANEUVERS** are further subdivided, they can aid you in developing rapid angle changes, increasing or decreasing **DISTANCE,** adding greater **POWER** to your strikes, and helping to nullify your opponent's actions. **FOOT** and **BODY MANEUVERS** are the primary ingredients that compose the **DIMENSIONAL STAGES OF ACTION** that was discussed earlier. Both types of **MANEUVERS** will be elaborated upon when the **FREESTYLE TECHNIQUES** themselves are described and illustrated.

I am gratified that the Kenpo system which I have developed teaches variables that include combinations of **FOOT** and **BODY MANUEVERS,** coordinated with arm and leg **BLOCKS** and **STRIKES.** Because of the multitude of **MANEUVERS, BLOCKS,** and **STRIKES** that are taught in *American Kenpo,* a countless number of variables are offered and *tailored* to student needs and abilities. Through dedicated practice, combined with understanding, variables become instinctive, as well as effective, during combat. Even angle and directional changes pose no problem to the spontaneous Kenpo stylist.

# TARGETS

**TARGETS** comprise the sixth preparatory consideration. They are the vital areas of the body which, when struck effectively, result in helplessness, pain, paralysis, or even death. Thus, having a thorough knowledge of these areas serves a dual purpose you will know which areas of your own body to protect, and where to strike to obtain maximum results.

For whatever reason, **TARGET AREAS** have often been a neglected facet of Martial Arts training. Since it is a known fact that having a thorough knowledge of precise locations can shorten combat time, study of **TARGET AREAS** is of vital importance.

Your efforts should always be channeled so as to produce immediate and positive results. Logic dictates this. Since some **TARGET AREAS** only require a minimum of force to cause helplessness, it is only logical that we learn where they are located. It would seem foolish to repeatedly **STRIKE** an area that would have little if any effect on your opponent. Contrary to modern thinking, strength, size, height, or weight is not a prerequisite in using your knowledge effectively.

Obviously the study of **TARGET AREAS** should also be coupled with the study of **NATURAL WEAPONS**. While knowledge of **TARGET AREAS** tells you where you can hit, knowledge of the **NATURAL WEAPONS**, along with methods and angles of executing them, tells you (1) what **NATURAL WEAPONS** can be expected from your opponent, and (2) what **NATURAL WEAPONS** you can logically employ to guarantee the best results.

# POSTURES AND POSITIONS IN RELATION TO TARGETS

To fully benefit from your study of **TARGET AREAS**, these vital points should be viewed from a variety of **POSTURES** and **POSITIONS**. While many of these **POSTURES** and **POSITIONS** are the result of natural combat **MANEUVERS**, they can also be created. Having knowledge of the effects of a **STRIKE**, and the reactions that stem from them, can help you determine the **POSTURE** and **POSITION** you may wish to create. It becomes apparent at this stage that **TARGET AREAS** alter with each change of **POSTURE** or **POSITION**. Consequently, your **POINT OF VIEW** will also vary with each change. To get a true perspective of your opponent's **POSTURES,** and **POSITIONS,** and the area that surrounds him, it is suggested that you employ the concept of **THREE POINTS OF VIEW.** To refresh your memory, the **THREE POINTS OF VIEW** concept entails viewing combative predicaments not only from your viewpoint, but from your opponent's viewpoint as well. Further, a third point of view that of the bystander who observes both you and your opponent should also be considered.

Technically speaking, a *fourth viewpoint* should be added. Knowing that your **STRIKES** can create specific **POSTURES** and **POSITIONS** on an opponent, you should consider the *viewpoint of a* **NATURAL WEAPON** *in relation* to its **TARGET**. Since your choice of **NATURAL WEAPON** is determined by the **POSITION, ANGLE,** or **DISTANCE** you are from your opponent, it is imperative that you instinctively select a **TARGET** and take action from the *point of origin* of your **NATURAL WEAPON.** Knowing that there is no one answer, prompt action is needed to produce immediate results. The *economy of motion* of your **NATURAL WEAPON,** in connection with your selected **TARGET,** is the key. However, sustained effect must accompany the **STRIKE** if it is to be considered *economy of motion.* If not, the classification changes to one of *wasted motion.* Do not forget to consider your own **TARGET** vulnerability, and take measures to protect them. Also, recognize the need to simultaneously utilize your **NATURAL DEFENSES** when **MANEUVERING,** for it re-enforces protection. Refer to Volume IV, Chapter 5 for more in-depth detail regarding specific **TARGETS** and their results when struck.

# CONTOURING PRINCIPLE

There are many aspects related to **TARGETS.** In learning more about **NATURAL WEAPONS** and the endless methods of executing them, I discovered that certain **NATURAL WEAPONS** seem to **FIT** the contours or surface areas of specific **TARGETS.** Astoundingly, the **FIT** is often perfect like a puzzle that no longer is mystifying when the right piece is added. Ironically, this perfect **FIT** can greatly enhance the effectiveness of a **STRIKE.** The **TARGET** takes the full impact of the **NATURAL WEAPONS.** As a result, not just a portion of the surface area is effected, but all of it.

When a **NATURAL WEAPON FITS** the **CONTOUR** of the **TARGET** that is being struck, it is categorized as **FITTING. FITTING** is one of the body contact methods that fall under the major category of **CONTOURING.**

# COMPLEMENTARY ANGLE

**COMPLEMENTARY ANGLE** is defined as "*a path or angle which parallels an attacking weapon, defensive posture, or a given line to produce maximum results.*" It may also be defined as an angle of delivery to insure contact to a specific **TARGET,** whether an opponent is attacking, maneuvering defensively, or is stationary. Examples of this principle can be found in Volume IV, page 72.)

# ANGLE OF INCIDENCE

As discussed earlier in the text, **ANGLE OF INCIDENCE** refers to your natural weapon making contact with your target at a perpendicular angle (right angle to each other) that will render the greatest effect. When the proper angle of delivery is achieved at impact your natural weapon has the capability of maximizing its force, thus causing surface concentration, and penetration to occur. Any contact other than a right angle delivery can proportionately decrease the effectiveness of target impact.

# SURFACE CONCENTRATION

**SURFACE CONCENTRATION** is an important aspect to consider if increased injury is contemplated. It is concerned with the impact force between weapon and target and the resulting stresses that occur. It follows the principle of a pin, or a nail, where the surface of the natural weapon being used is as small an area as possible in order to have a more penetrating effect on the target. While surface injury is at a minimum, the internal effects are much greater.

# PENETRATION

**PENETRATION** refers to the depth of your strike when making contact with your opponent's vital area (target). Strikes should be designed to terminate about an inch or two (depending upon the target) beyond the surface of the target. Since maximum velocity occurs between 70% and 80% of the way through your movement, it stands to reason that this is when impact should occur. The reasons for retrieving a strike rather than following through are two fold: It preserves your balance and economizes on your movements. After all, a strike that travels beyond the point intended is really no more than a *wasted push*. As previously stated, there are always exceptions to the rule. If a *lock-out punch* was strategically delivered it would be considered *useful, not wasted.*

# NATURAL WEAPONS

**NATURAL WEAPONS** constitute the seventh preparatory consideration. They can be described as being those parts of the body that can be transformed into fighting weapons. Knowledge of the many **NATURAL WEAPONS** should not only include "*what can be used*", but "*how it can be used*". Such study would also serve a dual purpose --you'll know what to anticipate when you are defending, as well as what your resources are when you are attacking.

Analytical study teaches that methods of executing **NATURAL WEAPONS** vary greatly, and, therefore, every effort should be made to familiarize yourself with them. Commit yourself to this and you will increase your **AWARENESS** considerably. If an opponent is limited in his knowledge of the uses of his **NATURAL WEAPONS** your chances of victory are improved. Consequently, contemplate all practical methods of execution. Most importantly, do not overlook the fact that new ones can be created.

All methods executed for purposes of injury are generally classified as **STRIKES.** The following information should help clarify moves that are classified as **STRIKES:**

# STRIKES

As discussed in Volume III, Chapter 4, **STRIKES** are described as being all *offensive moves* used to *hit* the *vital areas* (*targets*) of an opponent's body. They are basically missile-like moves moves that are explosive and accelerate like a projectile to make heavy or light contact. Depending upon the situation, contact may have various effects. It can cause temporary paralysis, injury, inflict pain, or under extreme cases maim, cripple, blind, or kill. These moves can follow linear as well as circular paths employing various parts of the arms, legs, or head.

There are several types of **STRIKES** as well as methods of executing them. Types refers to the natural weapons used as you kick, punch, butt, etc. Methods of executing them refers to the specific kind of force and/or path, direction, and position used in hitting your opponent. Naturally, application is contingent upon the opportunities that are available both from the standpoint of a target and a natural weapon. Please refer to Volume III, Chapter 4 for examples of the above mentioned **STRIKES.**

## NATURAL DEFENSES

**NATURAL DEFENSES,** the eighth preparatory consideration, are those natural parts of the body that can be used to defend yourself. Many of these **NATURAL DEFENSES** utilize the same parts of the anatomy used as **NATURAL WEAPONS.** What determines their use as either defense or offense is often the magnitude of force rendered, and/or that part of the anatomy used to strike. Moves used against an attack for purposes of defense are referred to as **BLOCKS.**

## BLOCKS

**BLOCKS** are primarily defensive moves employing physical contact to check, cushion, deflect, redirect, or stop an offensive move. On other occasions, they can be an anticipated defensive position, which, if correctly planned, can trigger a **BLOCK.** When executing a **BLOCK,** physical contact can occur: (1) when force meets force, (2) when force goes with force, (3) when force meets a neutral force, or (4) when a neutral force meets a neutral force. For further clarification refer to Volume III, Chapter 4.

## MENTAL AND PHYSICAL CONSTITUENTS

**MENTAL AND PHYSICAL CONSTITUENTS** constitute what could be considered the ninth preparatory consideration. These **CONSTITUENTS** entail proper methods of employing your mental attributes, synchronized breathing, how basic concepts and principles sequentially work, and how the universal pattern can be applied as a key to understanding motion. Sophisticated use of these ingredients and knowledge, harmoniously combined with those previously mentioned (knowledge of blocks, strikes, target areas, zone concepts, etc.), can generate, transmit, and focus phenomenal power in addition to obtaining precisioned accuracy. Please refer to Volume IV for further elaboration.

# A REVIEW OF CONTRIBUTING FACTORS

Let us review the contributing factors discussed in Chapter 6 that help us increase the effectiveness of our action. Increased effectiveness necessitates carrying *an erect posture*. An erect posture helps to maintain *good balance*. To enhance balance, you must learn to *relax*. Learning to relax enables you to increase your *speed*. Speed, however, must be coupled with *accuracy*. The development of accuracy teaches you how to *properly use angles*. Knowledge of the proper use of angles teaches you to be consistent in applying *economy of motion*. Economy of motion intensifies *precisioned timing*. Combine all of these contributing factors of motion and you will experience the ultimate in *coordination*. Coordination then *magnifies focus*, which in turn *re-enforces power*. Power is generated even more when you add synchronization of the *mind, breath*, and *body strength, body momentum, torque* (rotating force), *body alignment, back-up mass, gravitational marriage*, and *penetration* to those listed above.

# FREESTYLE TECHNIQUES

The following **FREESTYLE TECHNIQUES** describe how *Phase III* works. As you study these progressive patterns of attack take the initiative to develop patterns of your own. Utilize the *formula* as a guide in constructing logical and progressive patterns. Take special notice of how these **FREESTYLE TECHNIQUE** patterns engulf the four basic foot positions that can occur when facing an opponent. The detailed action also takes into consideration the varying distances that transpire, and the logical and progressive steps needed to remedy each situation. Coordinated with the patterns of attack are checks of all types to again acquaint you with methods of deterring or preventing counters from occurring.

**SPECIAL NOTE:** Many tournaments have been won by sticking to simple, basic techniques. The famous Joe Lewis was adept at executing a variety of techniques, but he chose to limit what he was capable of employing. His reasoning was also simple, the less he employed, the less his chances would be of getting hit. His strategy was to limit the number of target areas on his body without limiting his ability to score a point.

# SELECTED FREESTYLE TECHNIQUES

The following **FREESTYLE TECHNIQUES** have been selected to acquaint you with the way in which **FREESTYLE TECHNIQUES** are structured *progressively*. The *techniques* have been randomly chosen from the Yellow, Orange and Purple Belt requirements. It is hoped that from these *techniques* you will learn, and understand the *formulation process*. Comprehension of the *formulation process* will help you to develop an *independent and progressive approach* to learning **FREESTYLE TECHNIQUES**. This knowledge will only add to your development of *spontaneous reaction* during combat.

Similar to **SELF-DEFENSE TECHNIQUES,** there are four basic ways that you can face an opponent while sparring (see Chapter 4, page ??) -- *left to left; left to right; right to right; right to left*. The first leg position mentioned, whether right or left, refers to your forward or lead leg. The second leg mentioned refers to your opponent's lead leg.

Because most Americans are familiar with boxing, the *left to left* facing position is our first choice of instruction. Aside from being more commonly applied, it is a natural fighting position for the beginner. This, of course, would not hold true if you are a southpaw (left handed) or you are matched against a southpaw fighter.

Rather than give *names* to these *techniques* similar to symbolizing **SELF-DEFENSE TECHNIQUES,** alphabets and numbers are used instead to manifest **FREESTYLE TECHNIQUES.** Be sure to refer to the *keys* related to these *alphabets and numbers* since they correspond with, and define each of the **FREESTYLE TECHNIQUES.** These *alphabets and numbers* are part of an **EQUATION FORMULA** for sparring, comparable to **SELF-DEFENSE TECHNIQUES.** The **FORMULA** allows you to do the following to any given *base move* whether it be a single move or a series of moves. You can: (1) **PREFIX** it, add a move or moves before it, (2) **SUFFIX** it, add a move or moves after it, (3) **INSERT,** add a simultaneous move with the already established sequence, (4) **REARRANGE,** change the sequence of moves, (5) **ALTER** the weapon, the target, or both, (6) **ADJUST** the range, the angle of execution, or both the angle of execution and the range, (7) **REGULATE** the speed, the force, both speed and force, intent and speed, (8) **DELETE,** exclude a move or moves from the sequence.

We will now commence with some of the *"Left to Left"* **FREESTYLE TECHNIQUES** required for *Yellow Belt*. The *keys* to the techniques are thus described. The *alphabets* that describe the specific method(s) of execution are as follows:

B  (uppercase) -- represents the **BASE MOVE.** It consists of two variations. Both variations commence from a *"Left to Left"* fighting position.

**a** **(lowercase)** -- symbolizes the *first variation*. This *technique* requires that your left hand hook, grab, and pull your opponent's left arm diagonally down and to your left while simultaneously executing a right vertical punch to your opponent's face (photo a).

**b** **(lowercase)** -- symbolizes the *second variation*. This *technique* requires that your left hand hook, grab, and pull your opponent's left 1 arm down diagonally and to your left while simultaneously executing a right uppercut punch to your opponent's left lower ribcage (photo b). This punch is diagonal and parallel to the structure of your opponent's left ribcage.

Both variations require that you *check* your opponent's forward leg with your forward leg. This maneuver re-enforces an *angle of disturbance* and an *angle of cancellation*.

The *numbers* that denote **FREESTYLE TECHNIQUES** represent *body and foot maneuvers* that are necessary in gaging the distance between your opponent and you. They are synchronized with the two methods of execution mentioned above. The numbers are as follows:

**1** -- refers to pivoting (in-place) into a forward bow. This is a *body maneuver* void of a *foot maneuver*.

**2** -- refers to utilizing a *push-drag foot maneuver* when employing the two variations mentioned above.

**3** -- refers to employing a *front crossover, step out foot maneuver* using to the two variations mentioned above.

**4** -- indicates using a *front crossover, step out, step through foot maneuver* using the two variations mentioned above.

The following are the *alphabets and numbers* that symbolize the *Yellow Belt Techniques*:

| | |
|---|---|
| 1. **B1a** | 5. **B3a** |
| 2. **B1b** | 6. **B3b** |
| 3. **B2a** | 7. **B4a** |
| 4. **B2b** | 8. **B4b** |

**REMINDER: LL** -- **LEFT TO LEFT:** This signifies that it is your left leg (which is in a forward position) that is facing your opponent's left leg (which is forward). The first letter (in this case L) always refers to your lead leg (the leg that is forward). The second letter (also L in this case) refers to your opponent's lead leg.

# EXPLANATION OF
# THE YELLOW BELTFREESTYLE TECHNIQUES

**B1a** -- is the first variation, while *pivoting (in-place) into a left forward bow*. Photos 1, 2, 3, and a.

**B1b** -- is the second variation, while *pivoting (in-place) into a left forward bow*. Photos 1, 2, and a.

**B2a** -- "2" indicates that the movement to be used is a *push-drag*, needed in the event that your opponent is *a little out of range* or when your opponent is in the process of moving slightly back, while executing the *first variation* of the *base move*.

**B2b** -- indicates the *push-drag is used again*, but you are now to execute the *second variation* of the *base move*.

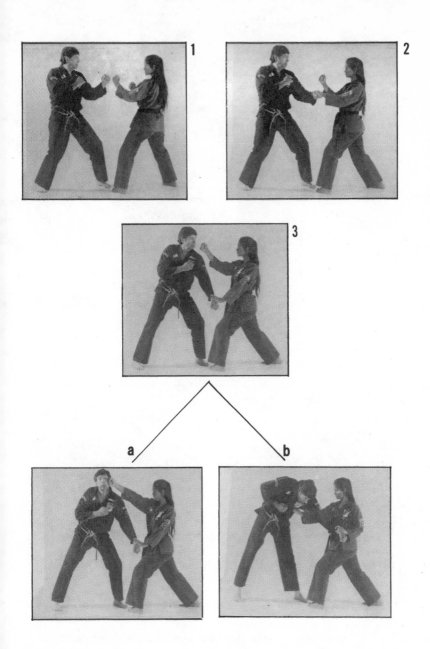

**B3a** -- "3" indicates that *a front crossover is executed while executing the grab*, followed immediately by a *step out* while you are executing the *first variation.* Photos 1, 2, and a.

**B3b** -- is the same application of the *front crossover, step out,* while you are executing the second variation. Photos 1, 2, and b.

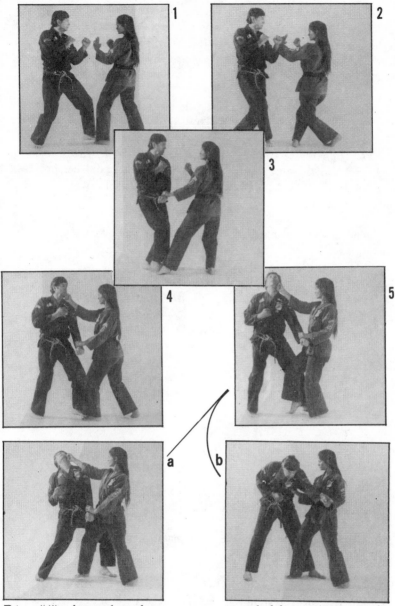

**B4a** -- "4" indicates that *a front crossover is executed while you are executing the grab, followed by a step out, then a step through* while you are executing the *first variation*. At this level, your right step through should position you *inside* of your opponent's *left leg*. (This is referred to as being *inside* of the *angle of entry*). Photos 1 through 5, and a.

**B4b** -- *is the same application of the front crossover, step out, step through* while executing the *second variation*. Photos 1 through 5, and b.

We will now commence with some of the *"Left to Left"* **FREESTYLE TECHNIQUES** required for *Orange Belt*. The majority of the *keys* to the techniques are identical to the *Yellow Belt*. The *alphabets* describe the specific method(s) of execution. Additional *alphabets* used to described the *Orange Belt* techniques are as follows:

K    (uppercase) refers to a **KICK.** In this belt category, K is associated with a **FRONT SNAP KICK** using the forward or left leg.

H    (uppercase) -- refers to a **HEEL PALM JAB.** In this belt category, H indicates that your grabbing hand (your left hand) is employed as a **HEEL PALM JAB** immediately after the **BASE MOVE** has been executed.

The following are the *alphabets and numbers* that symbolize the *Orange Belt Techniques:*

| | | | |
|---|---|---|---|
| B1a | KB1a | B1aH | B1aHK |
| B1b | KB1b | B1bH | B1bHK |
| B2a | KB2a | B2aH | B2aHK |
| B2b | KB2b | B2bH | B2bHK |
| B3a | KB3a | B3aH | B3aHK |
| B3b | KB3b | B3bH | B3bHK |
| B4a | KB4a | B4aH | B4aHK |
| B4b | KB4b | B4bH | B4bHK |

**NOTE:** Illustrated techniques will be indicated wherever applicable.

# EXPLANATION OF THE
# ORANGE BELT FREESTYLE TECHNIQUES

**B1a-B4b** are executed in the same manner as the **YELLOW BELT FREESTYLE TECHNIQUES.**

**KB1a** "K" represents a *front snap kick* to the groin using the forward or left leg. It is used as a *prefix* to an in-place body maneuver (pivot into a left forward bow), which is executed simultaneously with the *first variation* of the *base move.* Photos 1 through 4, and a.

**KB1b** is the same kick, followed by an in-place body maneuver (pivot into a left forward bow), which is executed simultaneously with the *second variation* of the *base move.* Photos 1 through 4, and b.

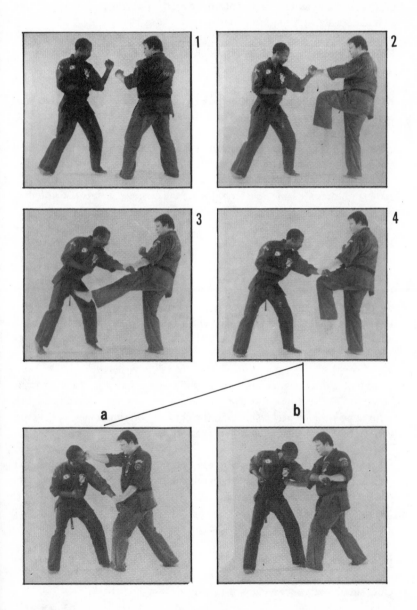

**KB2a** indicates the execution of the same kick. A *push-drag* is used in the event your opponent moves out of range after the kick; the *push-drag* is utilized simultaneously with the *first variation* of the *base move*.

**KB2b** is the same application of the kick and the *push-drag*, additionally using the *second variation* of the *base move*.

**KB3a** indicates the same *front snap kick*. A *front crossover, step out* is used to cover more distance, while executing the *first variation* of the *base move*.

**KB3b** indicates the same application of the kick and foot maneuvers, as you execute the *second variation* of the *base move*.

**KB4a** indicates the same *front snap kick*. A *front crossover, step-out, step-through* is used while executing the *first variation* of the *base move*.

**KB4b** indicates the same application of the kick and the foot maneuvers, as you then execute the *second variation* of the *base move*.

**B1aH "H"** represents a *heel palm jab* to the chin. Here it is used as a *suffix* to the *first variation* of the *base move*, as you execute an in-place body maneuver (pivot into a left forward bow). The left hand then executes a *heel palm jab*, while your right hand now acts as a sliding check on your opponent's left arm.

**B1bH** indicates the same in-place body maneuver (pivot into a left forward bow), while executing the *second variation* of the *base move*. It is immediately *suffixed* by your *left heel palm jab* to the chin, as you simultaneously execute your right sliding check. Photos 1, 2a, 3, and 4.

**B2aH** indicates that the movement to be used is a *push-drag* in the event that your opponent is a little out of range; this is simultaneously executed with the *first variation* of the base move. Immediately follow with a *left heel palm jab* to the chin while your right hand acts as a sliding check on your opponent's left arm. Photos 1, 2b, 3, and 4.

**B2bH** is the same *push-drag*, simultaneously executed with the *second variation* of the *base move*. It, too, is then *suffixed* with a left *heel palm jab* to the chin, simultaneously executed with your right sliding check.

1

a

b

2

3

4

**B3aH** indicates that a *front crossover, step-out* is used with the *first variation* of the *base move*. This is *suffixed* with a left *heel palm jab* to the chin, simultaneously executed with a right sliding check on your opponent's left arm.

**B3bH** is the same application of the foot maneuvers and the suffix, while using the *second variation* of the *base move*.

**B4aH** indicates that a *front crossover, step-out, step through* is executed with the *first variation* of the *base move*. It is then followed by your left *heel palm jab* to the chin simultaneously executing your right sliding check on your opponent's left arm.

**B4bH** is the same application of the foot maneuvers and the suffix, while using the *second variation* of the *base move*.

**B1aHK** "K" again represents a *front snap kick* to the groin, using the forward leg. It is used as a *suffix to the base move*. It is important to note that this *"keys"* the **FORMULA.** The "**H**" now may become *part of the base move* or remain as *part of the suffix*. Therefore, an *in-place* body maneuver (pivot into a left forward bow) is executed simultaneously with the *first variation* of the *base move*. It is then followed by a left *heel palm jab* to your opponent's chin, simultaneously applying a right sliding check on your opponent's left arm. Next **ADD** *a front snap kick off* the forward leg to your opponent's groin.

**B1 bHK** indicates the same application of the *in-place* body maneuver (pivot into a left forward bow), the *heel palm*, and the *front snap kick*, while executing the *second variation* of the *base move*.

**B2aHK** indicates the use of a *push-drag* simultaneously used with the *first variation* of the *base move*. This is then followed with a left *heel palm jab* to the chin, simultaneously applying a right sliding check on your opponent's left arm. Then **ADD** *a front snap kick* from the front leg to the groin.

**B2bHK** is the execution of the *second variation* of the *base move*, as you utilize the *push-drag*, the *heel palm*, and the *front snap kick*.

**B3aHK** indicates that a *front crossover, step-out* is used while executing the *first variation* of the *base move*. Then follow up with a left *heel palm jab* to the chin, while simultaneously using a right sliding check on your opponent's left arm. **ADD** *a front snap kick* using the front leg to the groin.

**B3bHK** is the execution of the *second variation* of the *base move*, as you utilize the application of the *front crossover, step-out*, followed with the same *heel palm jab* and *front snap kick*.

**B4aHK** indicates that a *front crossover, step-out, step through* is used while executing the *first variation* of the *base move*. This is then followed with a left *heel palm jab* to the chin, while simultaneously using a right sliding check on your opponent's left arm. **ADD** *a front snap kick* off the forward leg to the groin. Photos 1 through 6a, and 7 throught 11.

**B4bHK** is the execution of the *second variation* of the *base move*, as you apply the *front crossover, step-out, step through*. This is followed by the same *heel palm jab* to the chin and the same *front snap kick* to the groin. Photos 1 through 6b, and 7 throught 11.

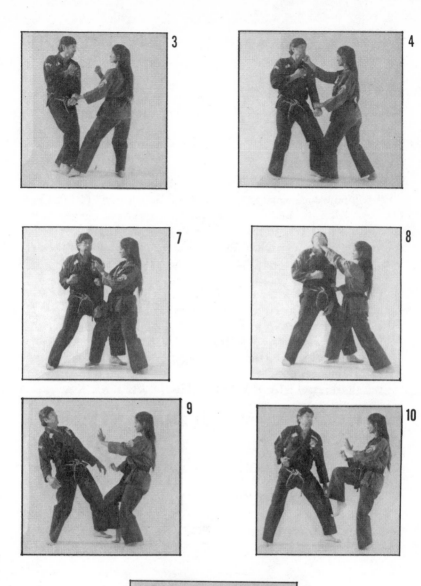

We will now commence with some of the *"Left to Left"* **FREESTYLE TECHNIQUES** required for *Purple Belt*. The majority of the *keys* to the techniques are identical to the *Yellow* and *Orange Belt* requirements. The *alphabets* describe the specific method(s) of execution. Additional *alphabets* used to described the *Purple Belt* techniques are as follows:

P   (**uppercase**) refers to a **PUNCH.**
bk   (**lowercase**) refers to a **BACK KNUCKLE STRIKE.**
r   (**lowercase**) refers to a **ROUNDHOUSE KICK.**
h   (**lowercase**) refers to a **HEEL** or **BACK HEEL KICK.** (Several variations of the **HEEL KICK** exist in the Purple Belt Freestyle Techniques.)
ts   (**lowercase**) refers to a **THRUSTING SWEEP KICK.**

The *numbers* representing **BODY** and **FOOT MANEUVERS** are as follows:

1 -- refers to an **IN-PLACE BODY MANEUVER.**

5 -- refers to a **STEPTHROUGH FOOT MANEUVER.**

6 -- refers to a **REAR CROSSOVER FOOT MANEUVER.**

The following are the *alphabets and numbers* that symbolize the *Purple Belt Techniques:*

| | |
|---|---|
| B5a | tsKrK |
| B5b | rKtsK |
| B5aP | * B1atsKrK |
| B5bP | * tsKrKB1a |
| B5aPbk | tsKB5a |
| B5aPhK | tsKB5b |
| B5aPbkhK | tsKB5aP |
| B5aPhKbk | tsKB5bP |

| | |
|---|---|
| tsKB5aPbk | rKtsKB5a |
| tsKB5aPhK | rKtsKB5b |
| tsKB5aPbkhK | rKtsKB5aP |
| tsKB5aPhKbk | rKtsKB5bP |
| rKtsK6bk | rKtsKB5bP |
| rKtsK6hK | rKtsKB5aPhK |
| * rKtsK6bkhK | * rKtsKB5aPbkhK |
| rKtsK6hKbk | rKtsKB5aPhKbk |

**NOTE:** Illustrated techniques are indicated by an asterisk.

# EXPLANATION OF THE
# PURPLE BELT FREESTYLE TECHNIQUES
(Illustrated Techniques Only)

* **B1 atskrK** -- indicates the execution of the *first variation* simultaneous with an in-place body maneuver (pivot into a left forward bow). The immediate follow-up is with a right *thrusting sweep kick* to the outside of your opponent's left knee. Without hesitating you are to deliver a left *roundhouse kick* to your opponent's groin. Photos 1 through 7.

* **tsKrKB1a** -- indicates a right *thrusting sweep kick* to the outside of your opponent's left knee followed by a left *roundhouse kick* to your opponent's groin. Immediately plant your left foot forward toward 12 o'clock into a left neutral bow executing the *first variation* of the *base move*, simultaneously execute an in-place body maneuver (pivot into a left forward bow).    See photos 1 through 6.

* **rKtsK6bkhK** -- indicates a left *roundhouse kick* to your opponent's groin followed by a right *thrusting sweep kick* to the outside of your opponent's left knee. Plant your right foot forward and immediately execute a left *rear crossover*, simultaneously with a right *outward back knuckle strike* to your opponent's face. Follow-up with a right *back scoop kick* to his groin. Before planting, execute a right *front crossover* and cover out in the direction of 4:30. See photos 1 through 10.

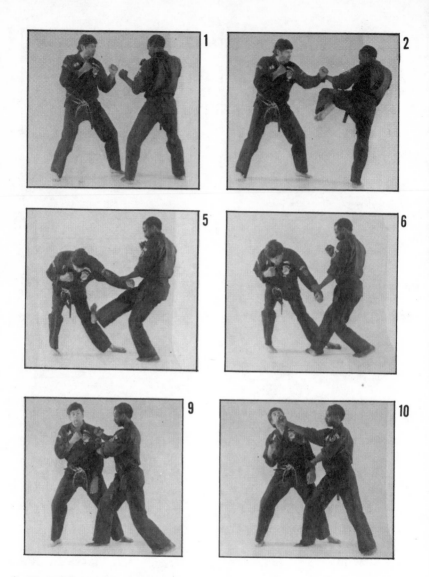

* **rKtsKB5aPbkhk** -- indicates a left *roundhouse kick* to your opponent's groin followed by a right *thrusting sweep kick* to the outside of your opponent's left knee. Plant your right foot forward toward 12:OO into a right neutral bow while executing the *first variation* of the *base move*. Follow-up with a left *vertical punch* to your opponent's face while executing a right sliding check down and onto your opponent's left arm. Without hesitating, deliver a right *outward back knuckle* strike to your opponent's face simultaneously with a left sliding check down and onto your opponent's left arm. Now deliver a right *back heel kick* to his body. Before planting, execute a right front crossover and cover out in the direction of 7:30. View photos 1 through 12.

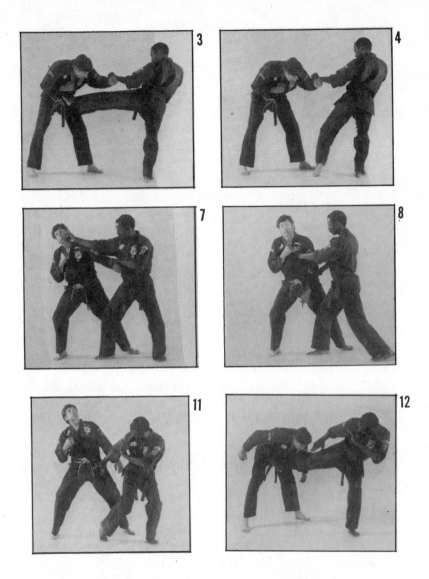

Although the Blue, Green, and Brown Belt **FREESTYLE TECHNIQUES** offer other concepts of interest, the illustrated techniques should suffice to help you learn to *formulate* working sequences of your own. While the number of **FREESTYLE TECHNIQUES** in the Blue, Green, and Brown Belt categories are numerous, they follow a logical pattern of progression. With thought and effort, you, too, can begin the challenge of *formulating* **FREESTYLE TECHNIQUES** that adhere to logic. Take up the challenge and run with it.

# NOTES ON THE YELLOW BELT
# FREESTYLE TECHNIQUES

1. The **LEFT TO LEFT** fighting position has been given priority since most Americans are familiar with these positions when they are boxing or street fighting.

2. To improve your *vocabulary of motion*, your chances of survival on the street, and your chances of success at tournaments, we highly recommend that you learn these same **FREESTYLE TECHNIQUES** from the **RIGHT TO RIGHT** fighting position as soon as possible.

3. When you are first learning these movements, try to get a feel for some of the favorable features that they offer:

   a. When action begins you cannot always choose the distance you would desire.

   b. Obtain knowledge of your hand strikes first. Practice your hand strikes while learning to *solidify your base* (stances). A *firm foundation* is much more important during the initial stages of learning.

   c. Move *quickly* and *unhesitatingly* when you are closing the gap between you and your opponent.

   d. The most effective punch delivered is one where your strongest arm is chambered in a rear hand position.

   e. If you can *cancel* your opponent's *leverage points*, he will not be able to strike *you* effectively.

4. The **WHAT IF** factors in **B4a** allows you a number of choices. You can plant your right foot *on the inside of*, *on top of*, or *outside of* your opponent's right foot. No matter what you may decide to use, it is important that you create an *angle of cancellation* simultaneously pulling with your left arm and planting your right foot. The precise placement of your right foot, while you simultaneously pull with your left arm nullifies your opponent's *height zones*.

# NOTES ON THE ORANGE BELT
# FREESTYLE TECHNIQUES

1.  Study your opponent's possible reactions to your strikes and maneuvers.
2.  Note that your checks, if executed properly are *Double Checks*. A *Double Check* is the execution of a single, simultaneous, or alternating delivery that restrains, hinders, or prevents an opponent from taking action from more than one leverage point.
3.  In "**KB3a**" it is a very practical alternative to execute the *front crossover*, then the *kick*, and then *plant* your left foot into a left neutral bow as you execute the *base move*.
4.  Create an *angle of disturbance*. The *angle of disturbance* is that angle which, when executed, does not necessarily injure, but rather upsets an opponent's balance. This can be accomplished by having your left hand pull your opponent's left arm while your lead leg buckles his left leg.
5.  Create an *angle of cancellation*. The *angle of cancellation* is a controlled angle which, when executed, places an opponent in a precarious position, thus minimizing or even nullifying the use of his weapons. See how you can cancel your opponent's height, width, and depth zones.
6.  Employ the principle of **WITH**; grab *"with"* a punch. This may be accomplished by having the rear hand punch begin the action so that the left and right hands are in *"Sync"* when contact is made. Employing this principle eliminates *Wasted Motion*, economizes on time, and generates the desired effect.
7.  Study the **FORMULA** presented at the beginning of the Orange Belt Freestyle Techniques. *Its importance cannot be overstated.*
8.  Develop *explosive action* in your movements. Do not *constipate* your motion by prematurely tensing your muscles.
9.  Be sure that your hands *do not flail* around during your maneuvers or while you are kicking. This will expose target areas on your body, waste time, weaken your strikes, decrease the accuracy of your strikes, and disturb your balance.
10. Be conscious of maintaining a *consistent head level* when you are closing the distance on your opponent.
11. Learn your Orange Belt **FREESTYLE TECHNIQUES** from the **RIGHT TO RIGHT** fighting position as soon as possible.

# NOTES ON THE PURPLE BELT FREESTYLE

1.  There are a number of methods used to execute the heel kick. You may thrust it, snap it, or hook it. This may be done vertically, diagonally, or horizontally. These probabilities result from the distances, positions, and variety of targets that you set up or may occur unexpectedly because of prior movements.

2.  Practice following a straight line pattern then have your partner circle you as you take turns working your techniques.

3.  Learn the importance of *critical distance*. *Critical distance* is that crucial distance that can place you and/or your opponent within striking range.

4.  Study your opponent's body reactions. Determine whether it is possible to execute your **FREESTYLE TECHNIQUES** with your opponent positioned on a horizontal plane (or varying angles of height), while you remain upright.

5.  Do not think of your **FREESTYLE TECHNIQUES** as simply Yellow, Orange, or Purple Belt Freestyle Techniques. Learn to blend them whether working them from *Left to Left* or *Right to Right*.

6.  Maintain *explosive pressure* when you are working with your partner. *Explosive pressure* refers to bursting, aggressive action that maintains constant aggression on your opponent preventing him from settling or retaliating.

7.  When sparring, blitz your opponent at all entry intervals. Learn to *control* all intervals when you are *closing* or opening the gap(s). (Deliver something on the way in, something when you get there, and something on the way out.)

8.  *Bumping* is a specialized method used to push your opponent away from you. Notice how *bumping* assists you to execute some of your **FREESTYLE TECHNIQUES**.

9.  Learn your Purple Belt **FREESTYLE TECHNIQUES** from the **RIGHT TO RIGHT** fighting position as soon as possible.

# CHAPTER 10
# CONCLUSION

This volume concludes my five volume series of **Infinite Insights into Kenpo**. While I am sad to see this series come to an end, I am nevertheless encouraged by the knowledge that a number of other books which I have written will soon be ready for publication.

I hope the contents of this five volume series has been of benefit to those who have read it. I must admit that writing this series was not an easy task. As I began this project, over fourteen years ago, I knew that I had undertaken more than just a normal task. The challenge was inviting, however, and I took the plunge.

The years I have spent analyzing, scrutinizing, creating, and developing the system I now teach have unlocked incalculable avenues of study. In my pursuit to analyze and develop many of the anticipated avenues, I felt rewarded when other avenues emerged unexpectedly. Because I was anxious to share my findings, I began to pursue logical approaches to explain many of my newly discovered concepts and principles. Realizing that proper communication is an important conduit to better understanding, I proceeded to employ analogies as tools to achieve my goals. I did not wish to lose sight of the need for clarity and understanding. The more I wrote, the better I was able to use analogies to clarify my findings. It became obvious to me that pursuing logical approaches to explain my findings brought realism into proper perspective. I discovered that concepts stemmed from using logic. Out of concepts, came theories. Theories blossomed into proven principles which helped bring realism into focus. From principles, emerged truths which allowed me to dissect, understand, and refine motion. Therefore, I write not to make converts, but to share concepts and principles overlooked by other systems. I further hope that capitalizing on my discoveries will allow those who are interested, more time to experiment and exploit other areas needing study. I am grateful that my forty years of experience has taught me to design Kenpo around a structural base. As is true of other art forms and disciplines, a structured base was needed to format Kenpo progressively, logically, and consistently. Our alphabetical and numerical systems both work on a basic structure. Although confined to rules and regulations associated with each, they are, nevertheless, consistent in application with endless variables to choose or format. Likewise, following a systematic base has resulted in Kenpo being propelling, viable, and void of stagnation. Following a consistent format has taught me to view motion and its variety of methods of employment, realistically.

# "SUCCESS"

He has achieved success who has lived well, laughed often and loved much; who has gained the respect of intelligent men; the trust of pure women and the love of little children; who has filled his niche and accomplished his task; who has left the world better than he found it, whether by an improved poppy, a perfect poem, or a rescued soul; who has never lacked appreciation of earth's brevity, or failed to express it; who has looked for the best in others, and given them the best he had; whose life was an inspiration; whose memory is a benediction.

Unknown

# GLOSSARY OF TERMINOLOGY

**ADJUST** -- part of the *formulation process* where you can calibrate the range, angle of execution, or both.

**ALTER** -- part of the *formulation process* where you can vary the weapon, target, or both.

**ANGLE OF DISTURBANCE** -- that angle which, when a move is executed, does not necessarily injure, but rather upsets an opponent's balance.

**ANGLE OF EXECUTION** -- any angle which, when an attack is executed, produces maximum results.

**ANGLE OF INCIDENCE** -- refers to your weapon making contact with your target on a perpendicular angle (right angle to each other) that will render the greatest effect.

**ANGLES OF TRAVEL** -- entail a more precise and acute viewpoint of direction. They describe *direction* as *degrees of measurement*. *Angles of travel* employ the "compass principle" where a student is made to visualize specific degrees on the compass to view motions of attack and defense.

**BACK-UP-MASS** -- the use of body weight that is directly behind of the action that is taking place. For example, (1) a punch delivered when the elbow is directly behind of the fist, or (2) the bracing of one finger directly behind the other when delivering a two finger chop to the throat, etc. BACK-UP-MASS is greatly enhanced when proper BODY ALIGNMENT is achieved. BODY ALIGNMENT gets MASS into proper perspective and allows the body to take full advantage of channeling weight and energy while traveling in the same direction (DIRECTIONAL HARMONY).

**BODY ALIGNMENT** -- this involves the placing of angles into perspective. It is the coordination of body parts in order to harmonize the angles they travel so that all parts of the body are in line to travel in one direction. This principle, when followed, automatically triggers the principle of BACK-UP-MASS where body weight enhances your action.

**BODY FUSION** -- a concept in which body parts move as a unit prior to relaying action to other parts of the body. These body parts are literally fused together in order to function as a single unit. Body fusion can occur any time during the course of a sequential flow of action.

**BORROWED FORCE** -- an opponent's force which is used to defeat him. This can be accomplished by going with the opponent's force or, upon occasion, going against his force. The concept allows your opponent's force to enhance the effectiveness of your action.

**COUNTER MANIPULATION** -- that stage of motion that is utilized just prior to employing the principle of opposing forces to its maximum.

**DEPTH OF PENETRATION** -- the concept of going beyond the point of contact when you are striking with a weapon.

**DIMENSIONAL ZONE THEORY** -- concept created to teach students of *American Kenpo* how to use their imagination to visually divide their opponent's body into vertical and horizontal zones (sections) as viewed from the front, side, or back. This in turn allows a student to subdivide an opponent into four basic zones-- height, width, depth, and zones of obscurity. Knowledge of this theory can also be used to keep your opponent's dimensions in check. Controlling your opponent's actions by restricting the use and versatility of his dimensions (ANGLE OF CANCELLATION), makes retaliation by your opponent considerably difficult.

**DIMENSIONS OF TRAVEL** -- are concerned with the *height, width,* and *depth of motion,* or the height, width and depth that can be created and controlled by motion.

**DIRECTION** -- as discussed in this book refers to the *direction* from which opponent's or your action may stem. It is one of the ingredients that make up the ANALYTICAL STUDY OF MOTION.

**DOUBLE FACTOR** -- it entails utilizing dual movements to defend yourself. These moves can incorporate any combination of blocks, parries, and checks. It also refers to sophisticated moves which are dually defensive and offensive. REVERSE MOTION is an integral part of this concept.

**ENGINEER OF MOTION** -- is that stage in a student's study where he not only can dissect motion, inspect it, understand it, and reassemble it like a *mechanic,* but extends beyond that point. At this stage he can rearrange, fuse, or create more sophisticated principles. These may stem from a combination of principles, but, nevertheless, they do take on a new perspective.

**FAMILY RELATED MOVES** -- the use of the same move or moves against a number of predicaments that are basically similar in context, but so often overlooked as similar in principle. For example, the answer to a wrist grab can (via slight alteration) be the same as a hair or lapel grab. The basic action is to control the opponent's wrist while striking against the joint of his elbow. The answer to a "rear bear hug", arms free, can also work if the arms are pinned or if the hug was converted into a "full nelson".

**FEEL** -- a word used to describe the foot or hand as it slides from one point to another. In the case of the foot, the concept teaches you to move your foot back ever so lightly so that it literally feels the ground when it is sliding in the hope of overcoming possible obstacles.

**FITTING** -- applying the shape of a natural weapon to fit the target being struck. It's like *fitting a puzzle*. The effectiveness of a strike is greatly enhanced when you are applying shapes that fit or match. This principle is known as the PUZZLE PRINCIPLE. It too is categorized as a method of CONTOURING.

**FOCUS** -- is the result of the entire body working as a unit at the very instant a target is struck. The concentration of mind (knowledge), breath, strength, and methods of execution must unite as one in conjunction with body momentum, torque, gravitational marriage, timing, speed, penetration, etc. It must be remembered that it is not just the concentration of weapon meeting target, but the entire body meeting the target as one unit that fully defines the term FOCUS.

**FORMULATE** -- the combining of moves into a systematized order, which when properly organized, develops into a logical and practical sequential arrangement.

**GRAFTING** -- is the combining of several principles within the flow of a single action. For example a strike may start with a hammering motion, but conclude with a thrusting action without disturbing the natural flow of the executed move. The term also refers to combining self-defense techniques without disruption in their completed or uncompleted state.

**GRAVITATIONAL CHECK** -- a form of CONTOURING where parts of an arm or leg rests on a particular surface area on an opponent's body to prevent him from obtaining height and leverage. This restriction can detain or prevent an opponent from taking action that can be detrimental.

**HAIRPIN** -- refers to a path of action that resembles the shape of a hairpin. It is a method of execution that elongates the circle and rounds off the corner.

**INTERNAL POWER** -- force from within developed via "*ki*" or "*chi*".

**LINE OF ATTACK** -- path that an opponent follows when he is attacking you. This LINE OF ATTACK can come from 12 o'clock, 4 o'clock, 8 o'clock, or from other numbers on the clock.

**LINE OF FIRE** -- path that a bullet follows when it is fired from a gun.

**MASTER KEY MOVE(S)** -- a move or series of moves that can be used in more than one predicament. For example, a rear heel kick, shin scrape, and instep stomp can be used for a FULL NELSON, BEAR HUG with the arms free or pinned, REAR ARM LOCK, etc. Or, an arm break can be applied to a cross wrist grab, a lapel grab, or hair grab -- application of the arm break would remain constant, but the methods of controlling the wrist would vary.

**MECHANIC OF MOTION** -- one who can dissect motion, inspect it, understand it, and reassemble it.

**MENTAL SPEED** -- is the speed at which the mind selects appropriate movements to effectively deal with the perceived stimulus.

**METHOD** -- is the underlying move(s) in which a block or strike can be executed. There are only two basic methods with which to execute a move -- linear (straight) and circular (curved). All the others are a variation of these. This is another of the ingredients that make up the ANALYTICAL STUDY OF MOTION.

**NATURE OF THE ATTACK** -- Refers to learning to: (1) identify, define and classify the types of encounters you may find yourself in; (2) thoroughly scrutinize the various methods in which weapons (natural or otherwise) can be employed; and (3) instinctively determine your choice of action in successfully combating the numerous types of encounters with which you may be confronted.

**OBJECT OBSCURITY** -- the use of your limbs to hide the action of another limb. For example, after a right two finger hook is applied to your opponent's left eye, your left hand can next use your right forearm as a track to zero in on the same target. Not until the left two finger poke is almost on target do you retract your right arm. The last minute replacement of weapons makes the second action obscure. This concept parallels the principle of TRACKING and is classified as a method of CONTOURING.

**OPEN END TRIANGLE** -- refers to the positioning of your body parts so that they form an opened end triangle. Use of these body formations help to funnel, wedge, trap, or prevent an opponent from injuring you.

**PENETRATION** -- refers to the depth of your strike when you are making contact with your opponent's vital area (target). Strikes should terminate about an inch or two (depending upon the target) beyond the surface of the target. Since maximum velocity occurs between 70% and 80% of the way through your movement, this is when impact should occur.

**PERCEPTUAL SPEED** -- is the speed at which the senses monitor the stimulus that it receives, determines the meaning of the stimulus, and swiftly conveys the perceived information to the brain so that mental speed can parlay the response.

**PHASE I** -- is an analytical process requiring that you commence with an *ideal* or *fixed* situation. This means that you are to select a combat situation that has been structured with a prescribed sequence of movements, and use this *ideal* technique as a basis to work from. In this phase, the term *ideal* implies that the situation is *fixed* and that the "*what if*" questions required in *Phase II* are not to be included in *Phase I*. It is the prescribed reaction of your opponent that completes the *ideal* technique.

**PHASE II** -- add questions of "*what if*". The tone of questioning in this instance slightly alters from "*what are they*" to "*what if*". "*What if*" you do counter these additional variables, how would your opponent react? At this stage of *Phase II*, you are programmed to thoroughly analyze probable variations to the model technique. Expected as well as unexpected opponent reactions are projected and evaluated. The principle here is that every movement has a consequence.

**PHASE III** -- this phase involves the actual application of your newly found alternatives to the original *ideal* or *fixed* technique. Knowing what can additionally happen within the framework of the *fixed* technique, teaches you how to apply your variable answers to a free and changing environment. It is at this phase that you learn to *formulate* your variable answers.

**PHYSICAL SPEED** -- is the *promptness of physical movement* -- the fluency in response to the perceived stimulus.

**PINNING CHECK** -- a *check* where you use pressure against your opponent's weapons to nullify delivery of these weapons.

**POINT(S) OF ORIGIN** -- the beginning, root, or source of any movement--the natural position or location of your body and natural weapon at the time action begins.

**POSITIONED CHECK** -- a *check* where you place the hand or leg in a defense position or angle to minimize entry to your vital areas.

**POWER** -- is the culmination of several principles -- the sum total of which maximizes the expenditure of energy. It is the magnification of force aided by concentrated focus. Its capacity is proportionate to the physical strength, force, or energy exerted, in addition to the speed it is rendered.

**REGULATE** -- part of the *formulation process* where you can govern the speed, force, speed and force, or the intent and speed of your action.

**ROLLING CHECK** -- a *check* where you use pressure by rolling against your opponent's weapons to nullify delivery of these weapons.

**ROTATIONAL FORCE** -- moves that use revolving action to contribute to power. TORQUE is a product of ROTATING FORCE.

**SETTLE** -- the gradual sinking of your body weight and height each time you alter the width or depth of your stance. GRAVITATIONAL MARRIAGE occurs with each height adjustment.

**SIGNIFY** -- a physical gesture using the fingers to indicate the number of the FORM that is about to be demonstrated.

**SLIDING CHECK** -- a specialized PINNING BLOCK that travels on an opponent's body by sliding from one leverage point to another. During the course of each slide, constant body contact is maintained (body contouring) to check for retaliation. This is technically a form of CONTOURING.

**SPEED** -- is equal to the distance divided by the time ($s = d/t$) it takes to act or move. There are *three categories of speed -- perceptual, mental,* and *physical* (body performance). However, although categorized separately in order to analyze what speed entails, these three elements, nevertheless, function as one.

**SPIRITUAL UNIFICATION** -- Synchronization of the powers of the mind.

**SURFACE CONCENTRATION** -- is concerned with the impact force between weapon and target and the resulting stresses that occur. It follows the principle of a pin or a nail where the surface of the natural weapon being used is as small an area as possible in order to have a more penetrating effect on the target.

**TAILORING** -- fitting moves to your body size, makeup, speed, and strength in order to maximize your physical efforts.

**TRACKING** -- is a specific way of CONTOURING that is used to obtain precisioned accuracy. It normally follows a limb of the body that is already on target so that the accuracy of your follow-up is guaranteed. For example, if you were executing a right two finger hook to your opponent's left eye, you should leave your finger on the target so that your left hand can follow the contour of your right arm in order to accurately poke the same eye. Timing in this instance is crucial. As your right hook leaves your opponent's eye, simultaneously have your left finger poke make contact to the very same target. Switching weapons at the last minute obscures the second strike.

**WEB OF KNOWLEDGE** -- A spider web pattern that is used to give priority to self-defense techniques according to the degree of difficulty expended in handling an attack.

To order additional copies of *ED PARKER'S INFINITE INSIGHTS INTO KENPO*, please mail your check or money order for $10.95 payable to:

ED PARKER
Post Office Box 595
South Pasadena, California 91030

CALIFORNIA RESIDENTS: Please add 6½% sales tax. NO C.O.D. ORDERS WILL BE ACCEPTED.
ADD $1.25 to cover postage and handling if you reside in the United States. Add additional postage for foreign requests.

## TO THE READER

The author will be most happy to receive your comments, including criticisms and suggestions. Noteworthy comments may be included in future editions or books of this series. If a reply is requested please send all correspondence, including a Self Addressed Stamped Envelope, to:

ED PARKER
Post Office Box 595
South Pasadena, California 91030

**Correct postage is necessary if you wish a reply.**